MASTERING

HAIRDRESSING

MACMILLAN MASTER SERIES

Banking
Basic English Law
Basic Management
Biology
British Politics
Business Communication
Chemistry
COBOL Programming
Commerce
Computer Programming
Computers
Data Processing
Economics
Electrical Engineering
Electronics
English Grammar
English Language
English Literature
French
French 2

German
Hairdressing
Italian
Keyboarding
Marketing
Mathematics
Modern British History
Modern World History
Nutrition
Office Practice
Pascal Programming
Physics
Principles of Accounts
Social Welfare
Sociology
Spanish
Statistics
Study Skills
Typewriting Skills
Word Processing

MASTERING
HAIRDRESSING

LEO PALLADINO

MACMILLAN

First published 1984
Reprinted 1985, 1986

Published by
MACMILLAN EDUCATION LTD
Houndmills, Basingstoke, Hampshire RG21 2XS
and London
Companies and representatives
throughout the world

Printed in Hong Kong

ISBN 0-333-35447-8 (hard cover)
    0-333-35448-6 (paper cover – home edition)
    0-333-35465-6 (paper cover – export edition)

CONTENTS

CONTENTS

CONTENTS

CONTENTS

PREFACE

Mastering Hairdressing is intended to help those engaged in hairdressing. It will be particularly helpful to the professional student hairdresser wishing to become methodical and efficient, and of special use to those taking practical examinations, or those concerned with practical hairdressing.

The book attempts to reduce the confusion of a variety of methods that exist to simple, straightforward ones. Once these are grasped, other methods and techniques can then be more profitably explored. It is hoped that this will prove useful both as a guide and a reference book.

Each chapter is independent of the others and can be read separately, but each contributes to the book as a whole. It would be wrong to suggest that all that needs to be learned can possibly be contained in a work of this size. The essential groundwork has been covered and it remains for individuals to create for themselves and decide how far they wish to progress.

I should like to take this opportunity of thanking my publishers, and all who made this book possible, for their help, forbearance and encouragement.

LEO PALLADINO

ACKNOWLEDGEMENTS

The author and publishers gratefully acknowledge the assistance given by the following in providing illustrative material for this book: The Institute of Dermatology, University of London; Messrs Wella (Gt Britain) Ltd; Messrs Teeda Ltd, London; Messrs Cavendish House Ltd, Cheltenham; Messrs Serventi Ltd, London; Messrs Walker Crosweller Ltd, Cheltenham; Barry Jackson; Christine Sammon; Diamond Edge Limited of Brighton. For photographs specially commissioned for *Mastering Hairdressing* the author and publishers wish to thank Kenny Fin of 'Kennady's', Newbury. For the cover picture of Hair by Michael of Michaeljohn for Wella, they wish to thank Wella Great Britain Limited.

Every effort has been made to trace and acknowledge all the copyright holders, but if any have been inadvertently overlooked the publishers will be pleased to make the necessary arrangements at the first opportunity.

HAIRDRESSING

1.1 HAIRDRESSING

This is the practice of curling, shaping, cutting, bleaching, colouring and decolouring, including the styling, dressing and care of the hair. There are many techniques involved, which need to be studied carefully to achieve success.

1.2 OBJECTIVES

The aim of good hairdressing is to apply what one has learnt and practised to improve one's client's appearance. It should be an enjoyable process for all concerned and will involve an understanding of human relationships, appreciation of what is beautiful, and a caring attitude.

Knowing something of the physical properties of hair and the variety of techniques available relating to it is vitally important.

Being able to communicate effectively in speech or writing is an important tool, and listening, understanding, expressing oneself clearly and interpreting what others are saying are essential to the practice of good hairdressing.

1.3 THE HAIRDRESSER

He or she must first and foremost be practically competent. The successful modern hairdresser must base his or her work on a thorough understanding of, and expertise in, the techniques of the craft.

For those who wish to become professional hairdressers there are many job opportunities, a useful place in society, and career prospects which are interesting, exciting and profitable. For the competent, a lifetime of enjoyment and success is possible, but this does not apply to those who wish to do the minimum, or to those who do not really care. As with any other

The 'good' hairdresser

business, for success in hairdressing it is necessary to practise, to endeavour to improve, and to care.

1.4 LEARNING HAIRDRESSING

Apprenticeship for a period of three years is the traditional method of learning hairdressing. With this method salon training is given throughout and added to by attendance at a college of further education, where a course of study leading to examinations and qualifications may be followed.

The two-year, full-time training course, usually at a college of further education, is an alternative to apprenticeship. At college all training is conducted in well-equipped salons where practical work and theory are carried out at the standard of a good salon. These courses usually work in conjunction with local and national hairdressing requirements. After completing the full-time course and examinations the student should be accepted as equal to the three-year trained apprentice.

There are schools, run on a commercial basis, where hairdressing can be learned. These present an easy, and probably most convenient, means of entry to the craft for the adult, mature student. Private school students study for periods of three to six months, or longer if necessary. After this learning period, with school examinations passed, they enter the craft. Some schools are well known for their results and are generally well accepted.

In addition to the initial training periods, further experience may be gained by attendance at a variety of manufacturers' seminars, teach-ins, etc. to familiarise students with the correct use of specific products. This is useful and helps the student to acquire a range of experience of different methods and products.

Recognised courses and examinations may differ in detail but they are all planned with similar ends in mind, by craft members and teachers who have studied the requirements needed by the competent hairdresser.

The examinations generally accepted in Great Britain are those of the City and Guilds of London Institute, the Hairdressing Council, and the Incorporated Guild of Wigmakers, Perfumers and Hairdressers. Most of these are available at colleges of further education throughout the country.

Prior to the more general provision of courses in local education authority colleges, a body known as the Academy Directorate regulated courses and examinations at private academies. This body still makes a valued contribution to the training of hairdressers.

1.5 THE COURSE OF STUDY AND TRAINING

At the end of this the hairdresser should know what to do, to achieve the results required. The better hairdresser will also know how to go about improving skills already acquired. The theory without the practice is rarely enough; an all round knowledge of practice and theory is ideally required and on this other skills may be built.

In the beginning the young hairdresser is faced with many small points which later are recognised as being fundamentally important. Among these are standards of hygiene, appearance and deportment. Poor personal *hygiene* is unpleasant and results in ill-health. Hairdressers must be clean and fresh at all times. Many clients will be influenced by first impressions and an unkempt appearance is not encouraging.

Deportment concerns the way one stands, walks and presents oneself, which is of major importance. The correct postures enable techniques to be applied with the least amount of effort and energy.

Attitudes adopted to the many people encountered daily in the course of work are influenced by the way one feels, thinks and acts towards them. In turn this affects the clients' attitudes, and their return as clients. It also affects the attitudes of those with whom we work and are trained. Those with helpful dispositions and attitudes will often find that help is returned readily to them. One must learn to live with people. It helps to listen and not be too talkative. It helps to be pleasant and courteous, but never slavish. One should try to be helpful, respectful and friendly.

Deportment, attitudes

What one wears, the colours chosen, the make-up used, reflect one's attitude to fashion. Generally, avoiding the extremes in appearance attracts respect, unless such fashions are a requirement of the type of salon worked in.

Punctuality is always important. Appointment systems are devised to make good use of time in the salon and a client cannot be attended if an assistant has failed to arrive on time. It is essential to be early for all appointments. The client should always be promptly and politely welcomed and attended. She must never be made to feel that she is a nuisance.

The appointment book must always be cared for and entries made correctly. Pencil is best used so that changes can be made easily. Mistakes will be reduced and entries more readily recognised. Record systems are designed to show what treatment the client has received on past visits. This ensures that the different processes can be accurately repeated. If these records are not maintained their value is lost.

The telephone, in the salon, is often neglected. When it rings there is invariably another client on the other end of the line and this person deserves the same prompt attention as a client arriving in person. Always answer clearly, giving salon name and number, and make a habit of recording all messages.

1.6 TRAINING

In a salon, this can begin when the young trainee has become used to the salon and its environment. In the beginning getting used to different people as quickly as possible is important and becoming used to the various tools and pieces of equipment is necessary. Exercises to help the co-ordination of hand and eye may be practised. Practice hair and blocks are used at first, progressing to live models later as work improves.

Problems with live models

Problems are usually encountered when using live models for the first time, since each head has its own peculiarities and more care and judgement is required. It is only when the preparatory work has been thorough, and properly understood, that other ways of work can follow successfully.

During training the work must of necessity be slow. Speed can only be developed when correct working methods have been achieved, but most problems can be overcome with practice, patience and guidance.

1.7 EXAMINATIONS

These all involve practical work methods which need to be attempted regularly, with guidance, until a degree of competence is achieved. Further progress can be made after successfully passing a basic examination by taking more advanced courses.

1.8 PRACTICAL HAIRDRESSING

Simply reading a book alone can never make a successful practising hairdresser and the intention of this book is to offer guidance, particularly to the new entrant. Each chapter concentrates on a specific aspect of practical hairdressing, and offers a particular method of approach. Each can be read, studied and followed separately, but some are best read and followed closely together. For instance, the chapters on cutting, styling and dressing are interdependent and should not be taken in isolation. In the beginning perhaps it is best to deal with the separate issues. The sooner these are put together then the better the results may be.

It is hoped that the words that now follow will contribute to the professional practice of hairdressing. If this book helps towards that end, then the hopes of all involved in compiling it will have been fulfilled.

HAIR AND SKIN

2.1 HAIR

Hair is the material with which the hairdresser works and on which hair-dressing processes act. Part of the hair is living and actively growing at its base but towards the tip it is virtually dead tissue. It grows out from the skin and is part of the natural body covering. The hair of animals is called a *coat*. When it is fine and kinky, and tends to matt together, it is called *wool*. Stiff hairs are called *bristles*, and if stiff and sharp they are called *spines*.

Human hair is quite different from that found in other living creatures. Some hair is tight, curly and woolly; other hair is either very straight or loosely waved. The scientific study of hair is known as *trichology* and someone who has studied trichology is called a *trichologist*.

2.2 WHAT HAIR DOES

Hair, like nail, horn, hoof, claw and feather, helps to protect. It does this in the following ways:

(a) by *cushioning* knocks and blows
(b) by *insulating* the skin
(c) by acting, with the skin, as a *warning system*.

Hair's protective property is well known to those who have little or no hair on their heads. A light blow on a bald head can be painful and even dangerous. Thick hair cushions a blow and even relatively hard knocks may be shrugged off. Hair holds a useful layer of air above the skin which keeps heat in and cold out. This ensures that the normal body temperature of 37°C (98.4°F) is maintained. In very hot conditions the hair retains sweat, which evaporates slowly and gradually cools the skin.

Hair and skin are very sensitive to touch and pressure. This enables them to act as an excellent warning system, by which the presence of any-

What hair does

Adornment

thing near them is detected. Hairs of the ears, eyes and nose are particularly adapted to this function. Movements of these hairs quickly detect the possibility of attack from without.

Adornment may be described as another function of hair. It is popularly known that a well-dressed person, with a good hair-do, feels good. Hairdressing has been found to be of value in the treatment of some mental conditions. Hairdressing may simply help to boost confidence of the individual, whose appearance affects the response of others. An untidy head of hair does not usually encourage favourable attention, but a well-dressed head of hair can be attractive, regardless of style, and does something for the person and others around. The young, old, sick and healthy respond favourably to good hairdressing, and the attractiveness of hair may well be considered as another protective feature.

2.3 KINDS OF HAIR

On the human body these are:

(a) the long hair of the scalp and face
(b) the short, bristly hairs of the nose, ears, eyebrows, eyelashes, armpits, chest, groin, arms and legs
(c) the soft, downy hair which covers most other areas of skin.

The largest amounts of hair are to be seen in the areas covering delicate underlying organs: the scalp hair which covers and protects the head and brain; the beard protecting the glands of the neck; the hair of the armpits which protects the upper parts of the lungs; the hair of the groin which covers the reproductive organs; the hair of the eyebrows and eyelashes which protects the eyes; the hairs of the nostrils and ears which protect these entrances. By the presence of hair in these particular areas, dust, small insects and water are prevented from entering the body openings.

When the soft, downy hair is missing from the face of a woman her appearance becomes hard and harsh. The softness given to the skin is an important part of beauty.

2.4 HAIR PARTS

The rounded part of the hair growing in the skin is called the *hair bulb* (see Figure 2.1). Where the bulb thins the term *neck of the bulb* is used. The hair length called the *hair shaft* continues above the level of the skin and ends in the *hair point*. The hair point of a new hair tapers but is made blunt by cutting. The root of the hair should not be confused with the root of a plant; there are no roots on the hair bulb.

The surface of the hair is called the *hair cuticle* (Figure 2.2). The cells

Fig 2.1 *Hair in skin*

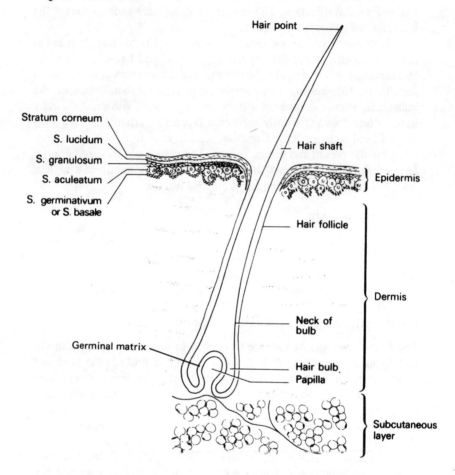

Hair point

Stratum corneum
S. lucidum
S. granulosum
S. aculeatum
S. germinativum or S. basale

Hair shaft

Epidermis

Hair follicle

Dermis

Neck of bulb

Germinal matrix

Hair bulb
Papilla

Subcutaneous layer

of the cuticle are arranged like the tiles of a roof, overlapping, with the free ends of these cells directed to the hair point. When hair tangles it is because these cells become locked together.

The condition of the hair affects the positions of the cuticle cells. When the hair is dry the cells lift at the edges. When it is in very poor condition the cuticle breaks and becomes very brittle. The surface of the hair cuticle fits into the lining of the *hair follicle* (Figure 2.3).

The *cortex* lies beneath the hair cuticle. The cortex cells are long lengths of tissue which form bundles of small cable-like structures. The cortex is the largest part of the hair. The natural colour pigment of the hair is found in large quantities in the cortex. A white hair with little or no pigment may have a large number of air spaces in place of colour particles (Figures 2.2, 2.4 and 2.5).

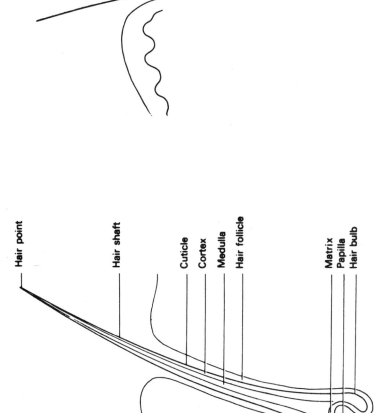

Fig 2.2 *hair section showing cuticle, cortex and medulla*

Fig 2.3 *interlocking cuticle and follicle surfaces*

Hair point

Hair shaft

Cuticle

Cortex

Medulla

Hair follicle

Matrix

Papilla

Hair bulb

Fig 2.4 *cortex magnified*

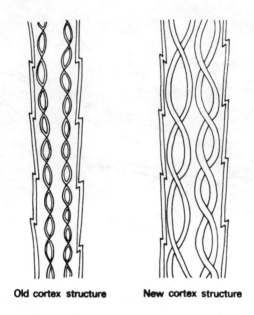

Old cortex structure   New cortex structure

Fig 2.5 *cortex - cell and colour arrangement*

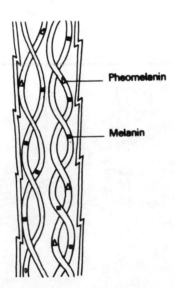

Pheomelanin

Melanin

The *medulla* (Figures 2.2, 2.6) is the central portion of the hair. It is composed of a number of long, soft cells, with air spaces in between. The medulla is not always present in all hairs. When the medulla is absent the cortex takes its place.

Fig 2.6 *medulla - magnified*

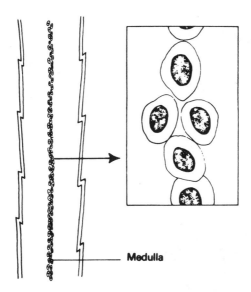

Medulla

The hair *follicle* is like a small tube in the skin. It lies at an angle with its lowest part deep in the skin. The lining of the follicle is like the surface of the hair. The overlapping cells of the cuticle interlock with the follicle lining (Figure 2.3), which holds the hair firmly in position. There are several layers of cells which form the follicle lining (Figures 2.7 and 2.8).

At the base of the follicle is the *hair papilla* which protrudes upwards into the follicle. The *germinal matrix* surrounds the hair papilla and together they form the growing point of the hair (Figures 2.9 and 2.9a).

The blood and nerve supply to the hair enters through the papilla. There is another band of nerves surrounding the follicle higher up. The blood brings its supply of necessary nutrients for hair growth, and also removes any waste products from the area.

When a hair is in the early stages of formation the cells are soft around the papilla and matrix. As growth continues the cells begin to harden until the pliable hair is complete. Hair then does its job of protection and eventually falls away to be replaced by new hair.

Fig 2.7   *interlocking cuticle and follicle surfaces. Follicle holding hair below skin*

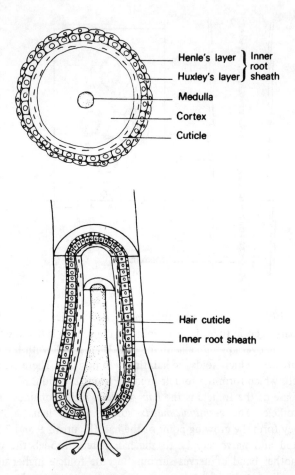

Fig 2.8 *cuticle surface and follicle lining cell arrangement*

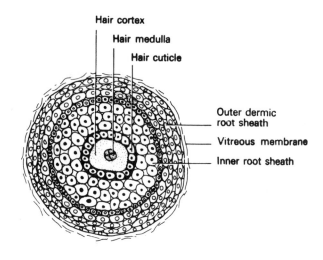

Hair cortex
Hair medulla
Hair cuticle

Outer dermic root sheath

Vitreous membrane

Inner root sheath

Fig 2.9 *Hair papilla*

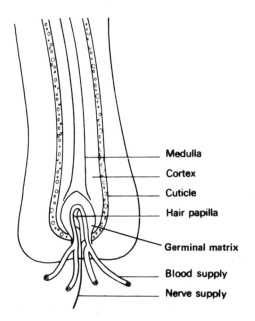

Medulla

Cortex

Cuticle

Hair papilla

Germinal matrix

Blood supply

Nerve supply

The colour of the hair is formed at the papilla and matrix. It is here that cells containing the colour pigment called *melanin* are formed. As the hair grows so the melanin is intermixed with the cortex cells. When there is little melanin grey or white hair results. This may occur after a long illness or when the papilla matrix area is disrupted. Although usually a sign of age, white hairs can be found in the hairs of many young people. Any colour change in hair takes place at the papilla and matrix. This is slow to be seen or noticed as the change is usually very gradual.

2.5 FOLLICLE PARTS

Other than the hair itself, these are (see Figure 2.9(a)).

(a) the oil glands
(b) the sweat glands
(c) the hair muscle
(d) blood vessels
(e) the nerve supply

The *oil* or *sebaceous glands* are situated in the skin surrounding the hair follicle. The glands have a number of sacs carrying the oil, or *sebum*, which passes through the mouth of the glands to the skin surface (Figure 2.10). The shine of hair in good condition is partly due to sebum. It lubricates the skin, makes hair pliable and flexible, prevents dryness, splitting or cracking, and helps to keep water out of the skin. Sebum has a slightly antiseptic action, and helps to prevent the growth of some bacteria.

If too much sebum is secreted the hair becomes lank and greasy. If the oil is allowed to accumulate and decompose, spots, pimples and blackheads may result. This is due to the oil becoming infected with germs. If too little sebum is secreted then dry, sore, cracked, and possibly infected, skin results. This may occur when degreasing chemicals, like washing detergents, are used repeatedly. Poor hygiene, e.g. not washing regularly, causes bad odour due to the decomposing sebum.

The *sweat glands* (Figure 2.11) are coiled balls of small tubes situated in the skin. The gland ducts, through which the sweat travels, are long, spiralling tubes which open at the skin surface. Sweat is mainly composed of water, but salt and other materials may be present.

Sweat glands are both secretory, i.e. the substance is made by the glands and passed out, and excretory, i.e. waste products from other parts of the body pass through the glands and out on to the skin. Sweat fulfils its cooling effect by evaporation; as the beads of sweat evaporate the temperature of the skin and body are lowered. If sweat is allowed to accumulate and decompose, bad odour and possibly disease may result.

The *hair muscle* is attached to the follicle and the underpart of the skin.

Fig 2.9 (a) *hair papilla. General skin and hair diagram*

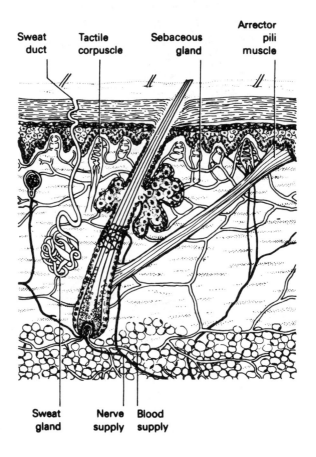

Sweat duct   Tactile corpuscle   Sebaceous gland   Arrector pili muscle

Sweat gland   Nerve supply   Blood supply

Fig 2.10 *sebaceous gland*

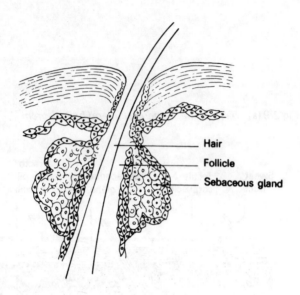

Hair

Follicle

Sebaceous gland

Fig 2.11 *sweat glands*

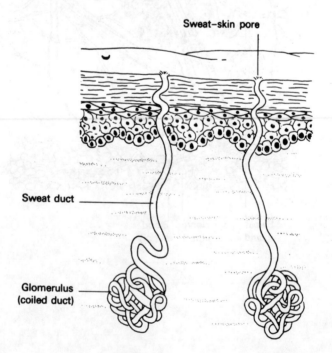

Sweat-skin pore

Sweat duct

Glomerulus
(coiled duct)

It is a small muscle which cannot be moved at will. When it contracts, the follicle and hair are raised to an upright position. The muscle lies at the same angle in the skin as the hair follicle. In cold weather the muscles contract to form 'goose pimples' on the skin, and the raising of the hair helps to contain a layer of warm air, which prevents heat loss from the body. In times of stress or danger the hair muscles cause the hair to lift, as a protective device. This is commonly seen in animals, for example, a cat's coat will rise if threatened by another animal.

Blood supply to and from the hair follicle is by way of small vessels situated at the base of the follicle. There is no direct supply to the hair other than through the papilla. The blood carries to the papilla the nutrient supply for hair and follicle growth. The transfer of these nutrients takes place in the papilla, where they are used up by the cell activity inside.

Waste products are transferred back to the blood stream through small veins. If the nutrient supply is interrupted by illness or starvation, a variation in the hair structure, a stopping of growth or cessation of activity at the papilla and matrix could result. Variation of the hair in thickness, texture and natural colour can only arise from changes occurring during the formation stage of hair growth. The blood is supplied from the heart to the head by way of the arteries, which subdivide to smaller vessels. Blood is returned to the heart by a series of venules and veins (Figure 2.12(a) and (b)).

The *nerve supply* of the hair and follicle is situated at the papilla and above the bulb of the hair, surrounding the follicle. Each of the parts of the follicle, except the hair itself, has its own nerve supply. The main nerves of the scalp and head originate in the brain and neck and by a series of branches and divisions they radiate to the various parts of the head. (Figure 2.13)

2.6 NEW IDEAS ON HAIR STRUCTURE

Better ways of photographing tiny objects are becoming known and it can now be seen that the hair cuticle consists of curved scales which overlap one another. There are approximately three to the complete circle, or circumference, of the hair, and there are a series of layers of cells.

The cortex consists of long, cable-like bundles, i.e. long lengths of cables intertwined to form unit bundles. All these cables are themselves bundles of smaller cables. These in turn divide again to form even smaller units of cable bundles. These different types of bundle are called microcables, photocables, and (the smallest units) protocables. The cable system in the cortex is continuous, branching and sub-branching from the larger to the smaller cables. The colour pigment appears to be distributed as was originally thought.

20

Fig 2.12(a) and (b) *blood supply to the head*

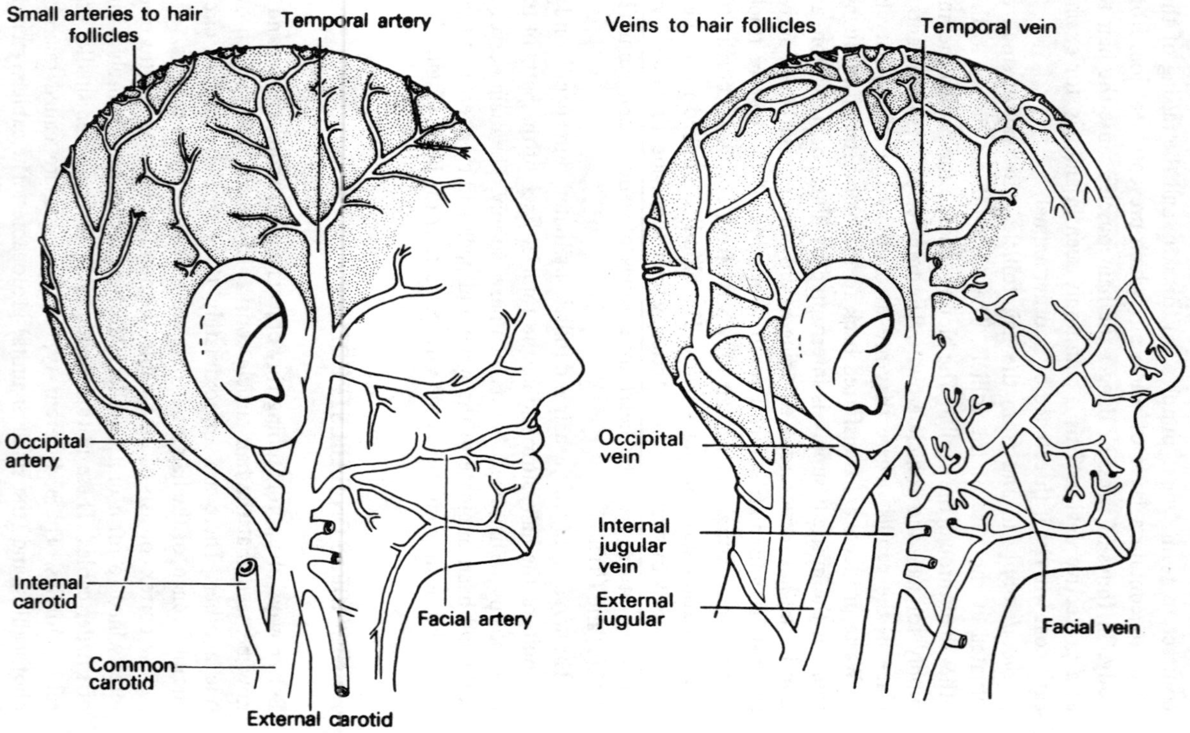

Figure (a) labels: Small arteries to hair follicles; Temporal artery; Facial artery; Occipital artery; Internal carotid; Common carotid; External carotid

Figure (b) labels: Veins to hair follicles; Temporal vein; Facial vein; Occipital vein; Internal jugular vein; External jugular

Fig 2.13 *nerve supply of hair and follicle*

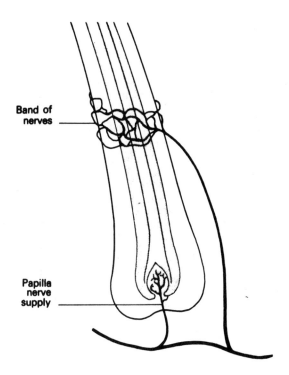

Band of
nerves

Papilla
nerve
supply

The medulla appears to be a soft mass of cables resembling spaghetti. The loops of the soft cables appear to form air spaces. Throughout each section of hair there appears an intertissue material called 'hair putty'. This apparently forms a large part of the weight of hair. When the putty is destroyed the hair disintegrates and falls apart.

It now seems that theories of hair structure will be reconsidered in the light of these new discoveries, and no doubt further research will take place.

2.7 THE SKIN

This is the outer covering of the body. It is one of the largest, and most important, organs. The skin contains a number of essential parts, and generally protects the delicate organs and tissues below. Contained in the skin are: the hairs, hair follicles, oil and sweat glands, muscles, blood vessels, nerves and sensory organs.

The functions of the skin are:

(a) protection
(b) heat control
(c) secretion and excretion
(c) sensation and absorption

The skin helps to protect the body by producing extra colour pigment, i.e. tanning prevents harmful rays from the sun damaging underlying tissues. The skin forms a barrier against germs and prevents infection. It is a flexible, tough covering, which repairs itself when torn.

Extremes of heat and cold are regulated by the normal hair function, the hair muscles and sweat glands, which help to maintain the body temperature. Secretion and excretion through the skin are maintained by the oil and sweat glands.

The *sense organs* are tiny units which lie immediately beneath the top layer of the skin. These units are well supplied with nerve endings which enable the stimulations and responses of the body to take place. Separate units convey the sensations of heat, cold, pain and touch.

The skin absorbs little and the depth of absorption is limited. Newer chemicals, however, have deeper, penetrating qualities. Water is rejected by the waterproofing effects of the natural oil of the skin, sebum.

2.8 SKIN PARTS

The skin is composed of several layers of cells and the lower the layer, the more active the cells. The top layer of the skin is the final result of the cell activity below.

The top layer of the skin is called the *epidermis*. It is the outer covering of the skin, and is divided into several layers. The cells of the top skin are hard and horny and arranged in an overlapping manner and known as the *horny layer*. There is little elasticity or colour in these cells, and the uppermost are in the process of falling from the skin. When the skin is wrapped in bandage for a long time the dead cells may be clearly seen on its removal as white flakes or strips of dead tissue. It is this part of the skin that is constantly being washed, rubbed or worn away.

Below the horny layer is the *clear layer*. This consists of clear, colourless cells. Sunlight penetrates through to this layer and activates temporary skin colouring.

The *granular layer* lies beneath the clear one. It is composed of layers of granulated cells which are softer than the hard cells above.

The next layer is composed of a mixture of cell types and is known by several names, the most common being the *prickle cell layer*. In the lower parts of this layer are found the cells which contain the natural colour pigment.

The *germinating layer* is the lowest of the epidermis. This is formed of larger cells which line the undulating base of the epidermis. It is sometimes called the *base layer* and consists of live, active cells which become the various layers above.

There is no blood or nerve supply to the epidermis, and all nutrient supplies come from below.

The *dermis* is the largest section of the skin and abundantly supplied with blood and nerve vessels. It also contains the units of touch, heat, cold and pain in its upper regions.

Underlying the dermis is the *subcutaneous tissue*. This is composed of loose cellular and fatty tissue. This part of the skin stores fat, and gives firmness and roundness to the body shapes. It assists in temperature regulation and acts as a protective cushion (see Figure 2.1 on page 10).

2.9 THE SCALP

This is the hairy covering of the upper part of the head. It extends from the forehead, above the ears, to the nape and is composed of epidermis, dermis, subcutaneous tissue, and a tendon sheet covering the head. The muscle part of the scalp is called the *occipital frontal muscle*. This originates in the occipital and frontal bones of the skull, with its insertion in the scalp tendon. Between the tendon sheet and the bones of the skull is a sheet of connective tissue.

2.10 THE SKULL

This is the bony case or shape of the head. It is composed of eight bones; the occipital; the frontal; two parietal; two temporal; an ethmoid and a sphenoid.

The joints of these bones are called sutures. The two soft spots on a newly born baby's head are due to the spaces between the bones which are called fontanelles. These later close up to form sutures as the baby grows. The lower part of the head, the face, is composed of fourteen facial bones: two maxillae; a mandible, two turbinal; two malar; two palatal; two nasal; two lachrymal and a vomer (see Figure 2.14).

2.11 HAIR GROWTH

In the unborn child the formation of hair in the skin initially takes place by a downgrowth of the epidermis, and an upgrowth from the area which is to become the papilla and germinal matrix. This growth continues until

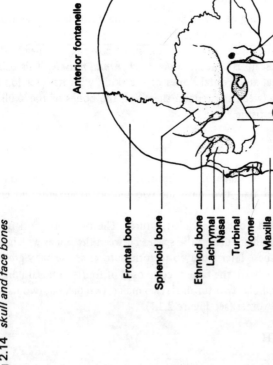

Fig 2.14 *skull and face bones*

Anterior fontanelle

Parietal bone

Posterior fontanelle

Occipital bone

Temporal bone

Palatine

Mandible

Malar

Frontal bone

Sphenoid bone

Ethmoid bone

Lachrymal

Nasal

Turbinal

Vomer

Maxilla

the first follicle is complete. The first hair formed is a lanugo-type (downy) hair. This is discarded before or soon after birth and the following hairs take the clearly recognized form they retain throughout life. The hair is replaced time and time again, until no more can be produced by the follicle. The fine, downy hair that remains after the normal hair has degenerated is called vellus hair. The fluffy type of hair to be seen on the female face is vellus hair also.

2.12 REPLACEMENT

Replacement of hair takes place periodically. As one hair is formed it grows, develops, remains in the skin up to six or seven years, and then falls, normally to be replaced by another. The life of an individual hair varies depending on variations in the body, mechanical activities and external factors inflicted on it. The growing stage of hair is called the *anagen* stage of growth. The length of this varies from a month to several years and it is during this stage that the length, thickness and texture of hair are determined (Figure 2.15). The next stage is called *catogen* in which no further hair growth takes place. Cell activity does continue at the papilla. The bulb gradually separates from the papilla and a mass of tissue surrounds the brushlike bulb. The hair remains but slowly moves up the follicle. The final stage is called the *telogen* or resting stage in which there is no further hair or papilla growth. The follicle begins to shrink, and separates from the papilla area. This resting stage does not last long and towards the end of the telogen period the follicle begins to grow down again. At the same time the papilla becomes more active, the old hair is moved further up the follicle towards the surface, and a new hair is formed at the new regenerated papilla and germinal matrix area. This starts the next anagen stage. The new hair pushes alongside the old, or the two remain in the same follicle for a short period.

Activation of the growth of new hair is not entirely understood. It is thought that germinating cells are passed down from the old hair to the papilla which activates the growth of new hair. There appears to be simultaneous growth of the follicle, and the new papilla, as in the beginning of first growth in the unborn child. After the resting stage a new growth takes place and, at an uneven rate, replaces the old. In some animals there is a more even rate of development. They moult or lose a large part of their hair which is then replaced. In humans this does not happen. If it did there would be a period when everyone would be bald, or partly bald.

Fig 2.15 *anagen, catogen and telogen growth stages*

Anagen   Catogen   Telogen (1)   (2)   Anagen (1)   (2)

The growth of hair is determined or influenced by:

(a) good health and diet
(b) age and sex
(c) hormone balance
(d) heredity factors
(e) climate and seasons
(f) physical conditions.

Health and diet: in normal health hair will form, grow, develop, finally fall out and be replaced, and for good health a balanced diet is necessary. A poor diet will affect the supply of the necessary nutrients, and will affect the growth of hair. If any of the essential food materials are missing from the diet, then normal hair development will be affected.

A normal balanced diet consists of:

(a) *protein*, found in lean meat, fish, cheese, eggs and milk
(b) *fats*, which are fuel for the body, from meat, fish oil, eggs and nuts
(c) *starch and sugars*, found in bread, potatoes, beans, cereals, honey, glucose and fruits
(d) *minerals* from table salt, milk, eggs, cheese, herrings, fish, liver and red meats
(e) *vitamins* from animal fats, fruit, vegetables and fish.

Age and sex: with age the working of the body tends to slow down. The skin loses its elasticity and becomes drier; wrinkles appear at the corners of the eyes; with some, hair fall and baldness occur. The chemicals which maintain the balance and sex of a person, and help the growth of hair and skin, undergo some change.

What is inherited affects the hair growth, but parents with good hair can often have children with poor hair. It happens the other way too: parents with poor hair can have children with good hair. A great variation is possible, but it is only a tendency that is inherited; habits, type of diet, general attitude, knowledge etc., probably have greater effects on the hair and skin.

Climate and seasons affect the normal body functions. There appears to be a seasonal change in hair growth. Spring and autumn are times when there may be greater hair fall and during the summer there is faster growth, which slows again during the winter. In many there is no noticeable change and the greatest effects of climate and season are probably due to changes in habits and diet.

Physical conditions, e.g. combing, brushing, etc. have been mentioned. Excessive restriction of blood flow, particularly when accompanied by excessive sweating, tension or fear, might affect normal hair growth. Hair pieces, if too heavy, worn for too long, and unclean, will soon have physical effects on the hair and skin.

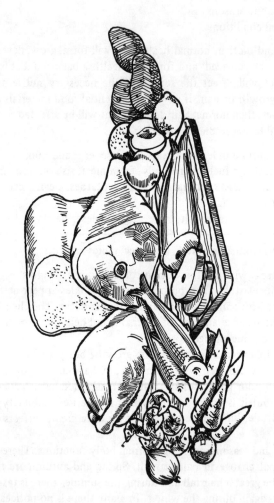

For good health, a balanced diet is necessary

A more complete understanding of the structure and growth of the hair and skin, which are part of the general body functions, may be achieved by a more detailed study of the body's systems.

EXERCISES

1 What is hair?
2 What does the hair do?
3 Describe and name, the parts of the hair above the surface of the skin.
4 How does hair grow?
5 What are the parts of the hair follicle?
6 What is the relation between the hair cuticle and the lining of the follicle?
7 What does the skin do?
8 What is the top surface of the skin called and what does it do?
9 What are the bones of the head called?
10 Name the parts of the scalp.

RECEPTION

3.1 RECEIVING THE CLIENT

The way the client is received is important. It begins when the client is first contacted at the reception area, on the telephone, or by post. Reception duties include polite and pleasant greeting, making appointments promptly, answering questions, and probably giving advice and information efficiently and correctly. Requests by the client for a variety of services, for information about costs and for general advice will be made. It is important to be able to respond to these requests or to call another person to deal promptly with them.

3.2 THE RECEPTION AREA

This is often the first thing the client sees. How well arranged it is and how clean and tidy it appears will influence the client's first impressions. An unclean and cluttered reception will never encourage a client either to stay or to return.

It is important that the staff's appearance and hygiene are professional and correct: this applies particularly to body freshness, fingernails and hair. Clothes and overalls must, of course, be fresh and clean at all times. The health and well-being of the client is essential and must never be endangered by unhygienic conditions. Good hairdressing in pleasant and hygienic surroundings is the ideal for professional service.

3.3 THE RECEPTIONIST

He or she should be attentive and ready to serve the client. All initial enquiries usually pass through the receptionist before the hairdresser receives the client, but in some salons the assistants deal with reception. Whether there is a receptionist or not clients must be received and welcomed into the salon as efficiently as possible with the minimum of delay.

The receptionist

3.4 THE CLIENT

The client is essential to business. Without clients there would be no need for staff. Clients attend for the services that can be bought, and for the way that they are carried out. This includes good work, pleasant surroundings, hygienic conditions and well mannered and efficient staff. Practical and professional craftsmanship is achieved by training, practice and time; so too are the skills required to deal with people. Some are better than others but the sooner staff realise that personal relationships are important to the building of business the sooner effective working is attained. The salon atmosphere will be pleasant when staff exercise goodwill and deal patiently with colleagues as well as clients. Disagreements and bad manners must be avoided if the salon is to remain harmonious. The client must never be aware of friction between staff, or ever be the subject of it.

3.5 HYGIENE

Good hygienic practices must be maintained at all times. Assistants should clear away soiled linen, hair, etc. after attending each client. Tidying is often carried out by the apprentice or junior. Cleaners are employed for floor washing and polishing, etc. When drains become blocked, or heating or water systems break down, it is the staff's responsibility to inform management immediately, to prevent damage and disruption.

3.6 CONDUCT

Conduct in the salon, particularly when busy, often becomes strained, but pleasantness and good manners are a must at all times. Hurrying rarely achieves anything but poor work and dissatisfaction and continually rushing work causes good skills and techniques to be lost. This results in repetition of work, loss of clients and loss of prestige. Steady, efficient work thoughtfully carried out usually maintains quality, clients and pleasant atmosphere.

3.7 ATTENDING THE CLIENT

After reception, attending the client means further inquiry as to what services are to be carried out. This should always be done unhurriedly and directly with the client. Clients' answers need very careful consideration, particularly when the requests seem to be almost impossible. The client may unintentionally give the wrong idea. She may request a hair style for

Attending the client

the wrong reasons or ask for something that to the professional hairdresser seems most unsuitable. It is the assistant's responsibility to interpret clients' requests: this should never be left to the apprentice. Juniors should learn not to express surprise at what may well be unusual requests; what is said must be conveyed to the assistant or manager for further discussion.

When it is clear what is to be done, make the client comfortable and prepare for the service to be carried out. Any delay must be explained. Do not allow the client to wait not knowing if, or when, she is to be attended. Working exactly to time is not always possible, particularly if clients with earlier appointments are unavoidably late.

3.8 PREPARATION

This begins once treatment has been decided. Assemble all tools and materials required. This enables the work to be carried out smoothly without unnecessary running about. Protective coverings are intended to protect and cover and spoilt clothes cause inconvenience and dissatisfaction, so make sure that all is in place before service is begun. A method of preparing the client is as follows:

(1) Place a neck strip or paper tissue over the collar or shoulders.
(2) Place a protective wrap carefully in position and secure.
(3) When washing the hair place a towel over the wrap or gown.
(4) Make sure all clothes are covered and client is comfortable.
(5) Check that all is clean: chairs, basins, etc.
(6) Remember that some materials act like sponges and should not be tucked into necklines.
(7) Make sure that chair backs are protected and that nothing falls between the chair back and the client to spoil clothes.

3.9 PREPARING THE CLIENT'S HAIR

This involves the removal of tangles and backdressing. Good preparation loosens lacquer, dust and skin scale from the hair and scalp. The hair will then become easier to comb, brush and work on. If preparation is not thorough it becomes difficult to carry out other services, as well as being uncomfortable for the client. Preparation of the hair is as follows:

(1) Loosen the hair with the fingers by gently teasing apart. This applies particularly to long hair.
(2) Use a coarse or widely spaced comb, called a rake. Begin combing at the hair points in the nape and gradually move closer to the scalp and higher up the head.
(3) Proceed from the bottom of sides and neck to the top front.
(4) All tangles and backdressing should be removed: do not pull the hair, scratch the scalp or break the comb while doing this. When untangled and loosened the hair is then ready for brushing.
(5) Brush the hair in a firm, smooth manner, supporting the head to prevent jerking. Start brushing at the ends of the hair in the neck, and gradually work up the head.

(6) When the hair is loose and flowing, brush in different directions. First from forehead to nape, front sides to the back, lower sides to the neck, and then in the opposite way.

3.10 COMBING AND COMBS

The best combs to use are the ones specially made for the purpose. These may be made of vulcanised rubber, tortoiseshell, ivory, wood, metal, bone, horn and various types of plastic. They should be non-inflammable, well balanced, pliable, resistant to hairdressing chemicals and easy to clean. Combs should be unbroken, free of sharp edges and mould lines,

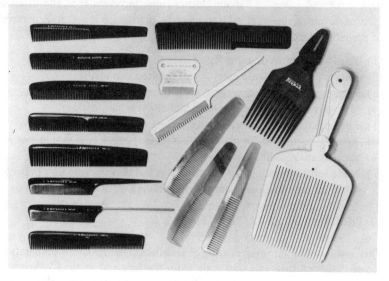

A range of combs

as a badly made comb can tear the hair and scalp. They could result in infection and disease. A broken comb harbours germs and is not easy to clean.

Some combs are made of material which make hair difficult to control. This makes the hair 'fly away' and stand away from the head. The comb for preparing the hair should:

(a) have wide spaced teeth
(b) be held firmly in the centre, with middle fingers on one side and thumb on the other (Figure 3.1).

Avoid straining the comb by holding correctly and do not allow the fingertips to slide down to the teeth points. The comb should be used upright,

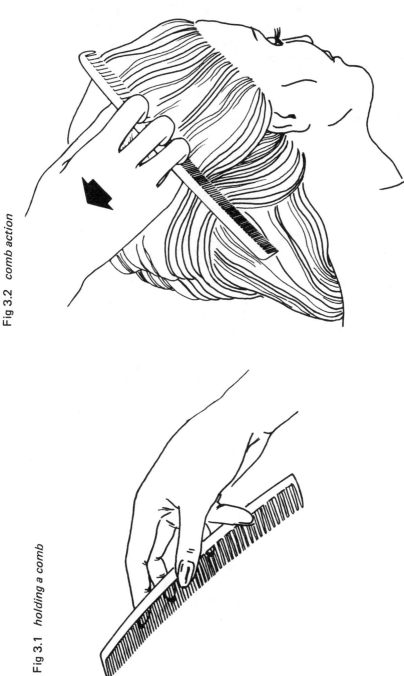

Fig 3.2 *comb action*

Fig 3.1 *holding a comb*

not flattened so that the hair is dragged. The comb should be used in a raking action without tugging. If combing starts at the hair points, tangles are soon removed. If started at the roots more knotting and tangling will result. Always support the scalp end of the long hair to prevent discomfort (Figures 3.2 and 3.3).

Fig 3.3 *position of hands, head and comb*

3.11 BRUSHING AND BRUSHES

Brushes may be made of a variety of materials. Commonly, good brushes are made from pigs' bristles or natural bristles. Others may be made from wire, plastic or rubber. They are made for a variety of purposes. Some are made for smoothing the hair, others for clearing loose hairs from the skin. The type to use is determined by what is to be achieved, and the texture of hair to be brushed. For preparing hair prior to other work, a firm-tufted brush which penetrates and disentangles is required. The brush should be well balanced and comfortable. The short, nylon-tufted brush is commonly used for general brushing and dressing. Nylon tufts if used too frequently or too long, as when used at home, can cause damage to the hair.

The natural bristle tufted brush penetrates, grips, helps place the hair, and is popularly used – particularly the short bristle type. Natural bristle

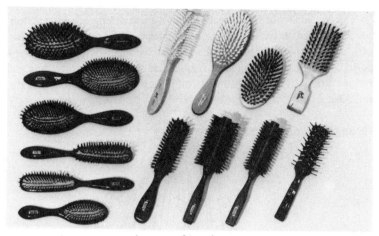

A range of brushes

is kinder to the hair. However, choice of brushes for the personal use of the client is different from that required for salon use. Generally, for thick, coarse hair, a short, stiff natural bristle, or nylon-tufted brush is suitable for salon use. If the hair is soft and thin, a longer bristle may be kinder. Apart from loosening dirt, scale, etc., the brushing action stimulates and distributes the natural oil and this is best achieved with a soft bristle brush. Dressing and styling hair requires a variety of mixed bristle, nylon or plastic brushes to be used. Personal choice of a brush is finally determined by its weight, length, size and comfort in use (Figure 3.4).

Fig 3.4 *hands and brushing*

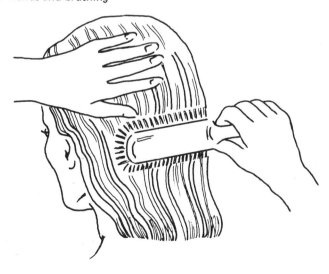

The brush should be correctly used in a smoothing, stroking action and never scrubbed or harshly used over the head. The brush should be turned with a rolling wrist action, and as with combing, the head must be supported. Two brushes may be used, one following the other, in a rolling action: alternatively, a brush and comb may be used together (Figure 3.5 and 3.6).

Fig 3.5 *using two brushes*

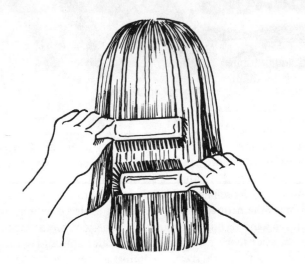

Fig 3.6 *use of brush and comb*

Precaution. If the skin of the scalp is torn or scratched with a brush or comb, clean the area with water and apply a suitable antiseptic to prevent infection. Only tools in good order, not likely to cause damage, should be used and always gently and correctly.

3.12 CLEANING TOOLS

Cleaning should be carried out soon after use. Tools should never be used on another person before being cleaned and sterilised. Loose material should be cleared from the brush or comb, they must then be thoroughly washed and placed in disinfectant, and then dried. Placing in a suitable disinfecting cabinet may take place after drying. Tools which have been placed in liquid disinfectants should be rinsed and dried before being used on a client, as disinfectants may, if allowed to touch the skin, cause irritation and discomfort. Some sterilising cabinets are made to both sterilise and store tools; others are made for disinfecting only. Care must be taken with metal tools when sterilising. They should not remain in sterilising cabinets, or liquid sterilisers, for too long, or the chemicals will spoil the metal. Manufacturers' instructions should be checked before using any sterilising method or chemical.

EXERCISES

1 What is meant by receiving the client?
2 Why is it necessary to prepare the client's hair?
3 What is the importance of personal and general hygiene?
4 What tools are used when preparing a client's hair?
5 How should a brush and comb be cleaned?
6 What is the difference between types of brush tufts?
7 Describe a method of combing long hair.
8 List the good points of a good comb.
9 How and why are protective coverings used?
10 List the points of care to be taken when dealing with a client.

CHAPTER 4

CURLS AND CURLING

4.1 CURLS

These are strips of hair spirally turned to produce a variety of shapes and effects. The curl may be set in wet hair and dressed when dry. Alternatively, the curl may be formed after heating and softening the hair and then dressed when it has cooled.

R.B. JACKSON

Curls

Curls and curling (a)

Curls and curling (b)

4.2 SETTING CURLS

Curls of various types may be used when setting the hair wet and there are many individual methods of curling. There are, however, some clearly definable basic types of curl (see Figure 4.1). To achieve a curl the wet hair is positioned so that when it is dressed it will follow the direction in which it was set. Basically, hair should be set in the way it is intended to be dressed. As the dressing loosens, the hair falls back into its original position. Dressing the hair opposite to the way it was set does not last long. Forcing the dressing, i.e. making the hair move opposite to the direction intended can become difficult for the client to manage. When more advanced, the skilled hairdresser can use force dressing to create special and different effects. Unfortunately, force dressing is often used to hide

Fig 4.1 *curl parts*

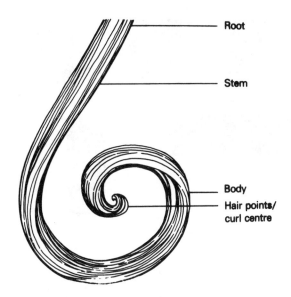

Root

Stem

Body
Hair points/
curl centre

mistakes made in the set by those who do not know the basic rules of setting.

Good curls require a degree of skill. Curls produce a variety of effects which are not easily copied by the unskilled. Curls produce individual shapes and contours which fit the head sometimes better than all-roller set methods can produce. Knowledge of the different curl effects and techniques is essential for the hair stylist. This can only be acquired by practice. Control of hair, hands, tools and client movements becomes easier with experience.

4.3 BASIC CURL RULES

These basic rules, if carefully followed, will allow most curls, regardless of method, to be achieved:

(1) Hair must be carefully combed and positioned.
(2) Hair sections must be neat and tidy.
(3) The size of the section depends on the length, texture and condition of the hair, and the effects required.
(4) The curl base of the hair section can vary in shape (Figure 4.2).
(5) The direction of the curl stem determines the direction of the hair section (Figure 4.3).

Fig 4.2 *sections for curls*

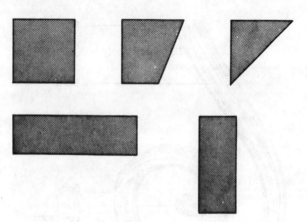

Fig 4.3 *curl stem directions*

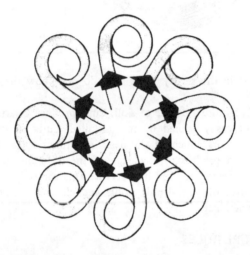

(6) The direction of the curl body determines the direction of the wave movement (Figure 4.4).

(7) Curls should be formed, without twisting, by carefully rounding each loop of the hair section.

(8) The curl should be placed in, or on, the curl base without distortion.

(9) Pins or clips should secure the curl without disturbing the curl shape or direction. Following curls should not be hindered by the pins or clips.

(10) When the curls have been placed they must not be disturbed by nets, cotton wool or ear protectors.

Fig 4.4 *curl body direction*

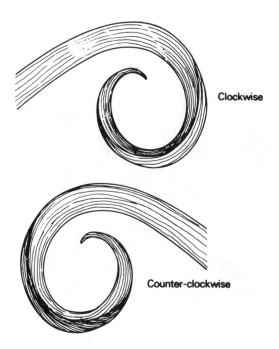

Clockwise

Counter-clockwise

4.4 CURLING

The curling process requires the co-ordination of hands, fingers and tools. Generally the tips of the fingers should be used with the body of the hands directed away from the head. This ensures that the work is not disturbed. Tail combs are used to divide and section the hair, and to position the hair strand on the fingers. The curl is formed by the fingers, or the curler on which hair is placed. Crêpe hair, cotton wool or end papers may be used to control the ends of the hair. These aids should never be so bulky that they disturb the hair. Pins, or hair clips, of different types are used to secure the hair in position for drying. A variety of shapes and sizes of rollers are commonly used to produce curl shapes. Other means of curling, e.g. curling wheels or root tensioning curlers are commonly used to achieve curl shapes (Figure 4.5). To protect the curl when drying, nets may be used to cover the set curls. Cotton wool or paper ear covers are used to protect the ears from the heat of the dryer. A variety of setting lotions may be used to bind the hair together. This helps to control the hair and produce a longer-lasting set.

Fig 4.5 *hands – curling position*

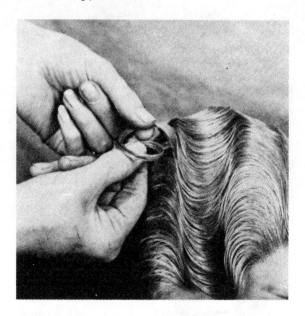

4.5 CURL TYPES

There are several types of curl, producing different effects. Most curl variations are derived from two basic types – the open or the closed type. These may be used lifted (standing up from the head) or placed flat. The position they are placed in determines the direction and effect.

Barrelspring is the name given to the open, loose, casual type of curl. It takes its name from the type of spring found in many hand haircutting clippers called a barrelspring. The centre of the curl should be open and the effect produced is softly casual. The curl is formed with each turn of the hair the same as the previous loop. The curl body is placed with the curl points above or below; above for flatness and below for fullness. The barrelspring curl produces an even wave shape throughout the length of each hair section. This curl may be used for reverse curling, i.e. where one row of curls is set in one direction and another row is set in the opposite direction to produce even wave shapes (Figure 4.6).

The **clockspring curl** is the closed, tighter type of curl. It is formed by each loop of hair being made smaller than the previous one so that the points form a small, closed circle in the curl centre. It is similar to the spring of a clock, closed because the points fill the centre, and a tight effect because the hair is wound tightly and becomes springy. When the

Fig 4.6 *barrelspring curl, set and dressed*

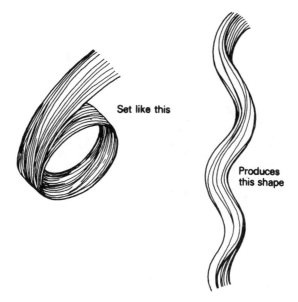

Set like this

Produces
this shape

clockspring curl is dressed an uneven wave shape is produced along the
length of the hair section. The larger wave shape is close to the root end
and the tighter wave shape towards the hair points. This curl is useful for
hair that does not hold its set well. It is used on greasy hair and in the nape
sections of some styles (Figure 4.7).

4.6 CURLING METHODS

The method used affects the result attained. A particular curl effect
required may determine the curling method. If the method of curling produces the wrong effect then the *method* is wrong – not the curl type. The
effect required is the main aim and there are generally several methods of
achieving it.

The effect produced by the curl is determined by:

(a) the size of the curl,
(b) the tension applied to the hair,
(c) the type of curl and method used.

Fig 4.7 *clockspring curl, set and dressed*

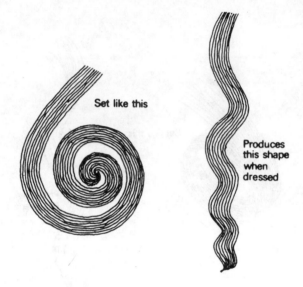

Set like this

Produces
this shape
when
dressed

Curling method 1. This may be used for tight or loose curls, big or small, with even or uneven wave shape. The guide is as follows:

(1) A section of hair is neatly divided. The size depends on the curl type and effect wanted.

(2) Untangle the section by cleanly combing through.

(3) Hold the section in the direction it is required to lie when dried.

(4) Hold the section, at mid-length, in one hand with the thumb and fore-finger, thumb uppermost.

(5) Hold the hair a little way down from the points with the thumb and forefinger of the other hand with thumb underneath. Turn the hand to form the first curl loop. This is a wrist action with the hand turning almost completely round at the wrist.

(6) On completion of the turn and first loop, transfer the coiled hair to the finger and thumb of the other hand where it should be firmly held.

(7) A number of loops are formed, depending on the hair length, in a similar way till the base is reached. The last loop is formed by turning the curl body into the base.

(8) The rounded side of the curl body should fit neatly into the rounded curl base.

(9) Support the curl with the fingers so that the base is not disturbed. It can then be secured without spoiling the shape.

This curling method may be adapted to produce both barrelspring and clockspring curls. The loops formed should be made larger or smaller, and placed in or on the previously formed loops, depending on the curl type required.

Curling method 2. Another method of curling is as follows:

(1) Hold the hair section in one hand with thumb and forefinger, thumb on top, 25-50mm from the scalp.
(2) With the thumb and forefinger of the other hand, thumb uppermost, grasp the hair 25-50mm away from the opposite hand.
(3) With a half turn, with hand nearest the hair points, place the hair in a loop.
(4) Transfer the loop formed to the tips of the thumb and forefinger of other hand.
(5) Continue to form the hair into a series of loops, transferring each to the other hand, until the length is coiled and the ends of hair are reached.
(6) The placing of the curl and the last loops of the curl are formed by turning, with both hands, the coiled length into the base.
(7) The curl is secured with pins or clips. If hair pins are used, place one through the curl stem and body, and another through the curl body, crossing and interlocking at the wavy part of the pins. Clips are best placed in line with the curl stem. This reduces hair marking, and does not interfere with curls formed or to be formed.

A method of rollering hair:

(1) A hair section, no longer nor wider than the size of roller used, should be cleanly combed straight up from the head.
(2) Place the hair points on the roller centre. Use both hands to maintain the hair angle and retain the hair points in position.
(3) The roller is turned, locking the hair points against the roller. The hair and the roller should be evenly wound down to the head. Pulling the hair from side to side when winding should be avoided.
(4) Place the wound roller centrally on the base from which the hair was taken.
(5) Secure the roller with a pin to prevent loosening.

Rollers, when correctly used produce good wave and shape with lifted effects. They are, however, often badly used and the results achieved are other than those intended. It is important to place the wound roller centrally on its base. If it is 'dropped' i.e. placed below the base, the hair becomes dragged, and flat hair rather than height is achieved. The hair

Curls and curling (c)

should not be dragged from either side of the roller, or rollers set too far apart, to prevent large divisions being produced which are difficult to blend. Avoid marking the head with roller pins. These are better placed by passing through to the next roller. The longer the hair, the larger the roller that can be used. Very large rollers in short hair produce weak and loose movements, if they can be persuaded to stay in the hair (Figure 4.8(a) and (b)).

4.7 COMMON CURLING FAULTS

(1) Lifting the curl base when a flat effect is wanted.
(2) Taking too large a section, particularly when hair is short, producing little shape or movement.

Fig 4.8(a) and (b) *rollers: (a) correct; (b) incorrect*

Correct

(a)

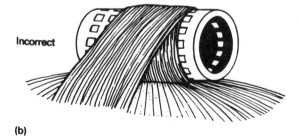

Incorrect

(b)

(3) Combing hair in one direction and forming the curl stem in another.
(4) Not rounding the curl body, and buckling the base when placing the curl.
(5) Bending the hair points back. This is commonly called 'fish-hooking'.
(6) Twisting the hair, causing it to move in the wrong direction.
(7) Distorting the curl base when securing the curl.
(8) Not placing the clip in far enough. This allows the curl to loosen and the clip to catch on nets, etc.
(9) Marking the hair by clipping across the stem. This applies particularly to bleached hair, or hair in poor condition.
(10) Taking uneven sections which causes curls to be out of line, producing uneven shapes.
(11) Allowing tools, or hands, to dislodge formed curls.
(12) Not using the tips of the fingers, or carefully lining up each curled loop. This produces untidy, uneven effects.

4.8 BASES AND SECTIONS

Bases and sections of curls can be of various shapes, e.g. oblong, square or triangular. These are determined by the type of curl used, and the direction in which it is intended to place the hair. Barrelspring curls require slightly oblong bases. Roller curls require wider oblong bases, and clockspring curls require square bases. Triangular bases are used with part standup type curls. Oblong and square bases are the most commonly used.

Practising the two basic curl types is to be encouraged before attempting to set. Competently placing smooth, flat or round, neat and tidy curls, in varying positions will soon allow speedy completion of a good set.

There are two directions in which a flat curl may be formed: clockwise and counter-clockwise. The clockwise curl moves in the direction of the hands of a clock. Counter-clockwise curls move in the opposite direction. Roller, and stand-up curls, are formed, basically, with their stems directed up from the head.

4.9 CURL EXERCISES

(1) Commencing at the top centre part of the head, form a complete circle of barrelspring curls. Make the curl stems long enough for the circle to be completed. Follow this with an outer circle of curls, close to the first, but moving in the opposite direction (Figure 4.9).
(2) Form two straight rows of barrelspring curls, one row clockwise, the other counter-clockwise, across the back of the head or practice block. When dry, simply brush through and well-formed waves should result. This exercise may be applied in various ways for styling (Figure 4.10).

Fig 4.9 *circle of curls*

Fig 4.10 *two rows of reverse curls*

4.10 SETTING

Setting is the use of a variety of curls in patterns that produce different effects. The average good set requires two or three different types of curl, but there should always be enough of each type to complete a shape or movement.

The combinations of curls, shape and movements required, and the curling methods used, must be considered when designing the set. The final shape produced will depend on this. Some sections may need to be lifted, either partly or fully. Other style effects require flat, curly, loose or tight, straight or waved hair, in different parts of the head. The basic curls, and variations of them, are used to produce the effects wanted.

Variations of the barrelspring type curl are: the roller-type curl, the stand-up curl, the part-lifted curl, the barrel curl and the reverse curl. The barrelspring curl can be used to produce tight or loose and small or large, effects by altering the size of the curl.

The roller, stand-up, part-lifted and barrel-type curl are formed similarly. All have their base stems directed up from the head, and produce height and fullness. The *roller curl* produces the effects of several curls in one area, but without the individual movements of separate curls. The main difference between these curls is the amount of tension used and their size.

The *stand-up curl,* sometimes called the cascade, is formed on an oblong base, longer than its width, with an open centre and a lifted base. A high, soft and casual effect is produced. Its advantage is the individual movement and direction given (Figure 4.11).

Fig 4.11 *cascade or stand-up curl*

The *barrel curl* is formed on a smaller base than that used by a roller, and its variation of stem direction produces interesting shapes. The curl is formed from the points, or held in the centre and the points placed on to its base. A clip retains the lifted base and curl position. Barrel curls are wider than cascade, and narrower than roller curls (Figure 4.12).

The *part stand-up curl* is a particularly useful type. Its angle of stem can be varied between that produced by the cascade and flat barrelspring curls. The clip secures the stem angle. This curl is best used where varied lift is required and movements graduating from height to flatness are wanted (Figure 4.13).

Fig 4.12 *barrel curl*

Fig 4.13 *part stand-up curl*

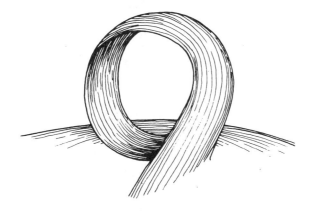

The *reverse curl* is used in an alternating manner, i.e. one row of curls clockwise, the next placed counter-clockwise. This produces shape and movement (Figure 4.14).

Other curl variations include the following: the *root tensioned curl*, known as a *French curl*, is formed by wrapping the hair ribbon-like around the finger with the base tensed and firmly held. A lifted base with softly-waved lengths is the effect produced, which allows hair to be dressed in various directions. Several curl formers have been produced to create these effects (Figure 4.15).

The *crescent curl* is used to produce flat kiss-curl effects on the hairline, wispy shapes at the sides and flicked ducktail shapes at the back and nape. It is formed by cleanly combing the stem direction, making a large open centre and securing the points, without fish-hooking (Figure 4.16).

Fig 4.14   *reverse curls*

Fig 4.15 *root-tensioned curl*

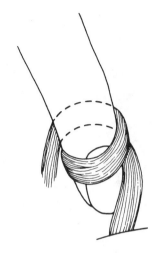

Fig 4.16 *crescent curl*

The *ringlet curl* produces pleasing shapes. It features in many modern dressings and may be formed in several ways. If formed from the points it will hang loosely since most of the tension is placed at the points. It may be formed spirally from the roots by winding the hair on to thin rollers or curlers. The ends may be secured with crêpe hair, end-papers or string (Figure 4.17). Curling ringlets with heated irons was, and is, popularly done. Forming from the roots or the points, by rolling and wrapping on to warm irons, produces quick, pleasing results (Figure 4.18).

Curl gadgets of different types, and varied shapes of curlers, have been devised and are used to produce different curl effects. Most of them vary the curling method rather than the curl type. Curl platforms, which raised curl stems and held rollers, and circular curling wheels, enjoyed a measure of popularity. Useful as these are they do not take the place of curling techniques produced by the fingers and simple tools.

Fig 4.17 *ringlets*

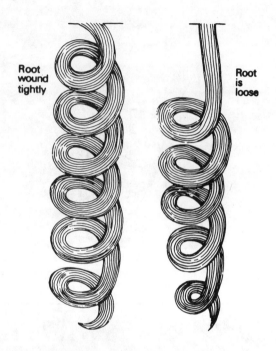

Root
wound
tightly

Root
is
loose

Fig 4.18 *ringlet formation using irons*

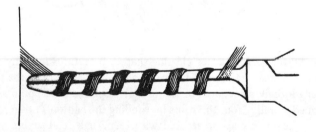

4.11 THE STEAM SET

Steam setting is a method of placing dry hair into set, steaming, cooling and then dressing in the normal way. The hair is first washed and dried and a net may be used to protect the set when drying.

After drying, the hair should be set in the same way as if it were wet. Curl control and placing is more difficult when the hair is dry, but it becomes easier with practice. The set hair is placed under a steamer for three minutes. This makes the hair damp and allows it to take the shape of the formed curl. The set is then placed under the dryer again, but for five minutes only, and the hair is ready for dressing as soon as it has cooled.

The steam set enables a quick shape to be produced with shiny, easy-to-dress hair. The normal drying time is considerably reduced and the time taken for the complete set and dressing is halved. Long hair may be set and dressed in thirty minutes.

4.12 HEATED ROLLER SETTING

This technique is similar to curling with heated irons, the hair being rolled or curled and positioned on the heated rollers. The hair is softened by the heat and takes the shape in which it is moulded. Allow the hair to cool before dressing. Applied to hair after washing and drying, or to dry hair if it is not greasy, it becomes a useful and quick method of setting.

4.13 BLOW STYLING

A method of shaping the hair into style using the heat of a hand hair dryer, combined with combs and brushes. In essence, the hair is softened by the heated air stream and moulded into position by the movements of brush and comb. It is important to make sure that the hair is fully dry before completion or the shape will be lost and the finish affected.

4.14 PLI

This term is derived from the French *mis-en-pli*, which means to put in set or position. It is commonly used in place of the word 'set'. The set when wet is often referred to as the wet pli and the dry pli when it is dried and dressed.

4.15 SETTING LOTIONS

These are used to set the hair in position, and help to produce a longer-lasting shape. The newer setting lotions have the advantage of softening the hair, allowing it to be moulded into shape, preventing the hair becoming flyaway when dressed, and coating the hair to resist damp, so retaining the hair set longer. Other lotions used for blow styling help to give the hair more body as well as helping to retain the wave positions.

The hair must be towel dried before applying these lotions, as too much water left on the hair will dilute the lotion, reduce its effects, and make it flake when dry. Colour or conditioners are added to some lotions, and others are designed to correct over-greasy or dry hair. Always read the instructions for the lotion's use before applying.

4.16 DRESSING THE SET

The final shape in which the hair is dressed should be kept in mind throughout the process of setting. The direction in which each curl stem moves, the way each curl body turns, the combination of curl types and methods of curling used, all help to form lines, curves and the patterns which make the final shape. A single line placed by means of a curl stem in a certain direction will have its effect in the final dressing.

The dressing of hair is considered to require a measure of artistic appreciation and imagination. To set hair in certain positions to achieve an imagined shape when dressed does require a great deal of thought. Often little artistry is used in setting, or the set is completely disregarded, relying solely on the ability to dress the positions required. The basis of good hair shape is determined by the set, and the ability to dress should be used to improve the set. Unless the foundations are well laid or set, extra dressing will be necessary, more time needed to correct lack of movement, and unpractical, difficult shapes result.

Ideally, the final dressings should be planned and set for. The look, feel and impression created are important. Both thought and understanding are necessary for success; to know in which direction this or that curl should be placed to achieve a certain effect, is a matter of time, practice and experience. The effects of height, depth and width of the curls set can only be appreciated when the ability to form them has been mastered. The line, form and the look created by them may be fully understood when the young stylist has achieved some artistic appreciation.

Some people are able to absorb from everyday happenings impressions that influence their manner and work. Some are able to create originally, seemingly out of thin air; others have to work hard to produce anything different. There are some who, unfortunately, do not begin to see or understand the important links between the set and the dressing. Nor can they plan for the imagined shape with a planned set or achieve the satisfaction of attainment. Again, it must be stressed that a variety of curls and curling form the foundation for the final dressing. Practised use of the varied effects can produce an almost infinite range of creative dressings. Using the same curl in the same way does not help to produce original or varied effects. Learning to use the techniques and effects available makes for more interesting and acceptable results.

EXERCISES

1 What is a curl as used in hairdressing?
2 Describe a method of curling.
3 What are the main parts of a curl?
4 Why are curls used in setting?
5 What determines the direction of a curl?
6 List the common curling faults.
7 What is meant by 'forced dressing'?
8 Describe five rules of curling.
9 How, and why, should a roller curl be used correctly?
10 How does tension affect the curl?

CHAPTER 5

HAIR WASHING

5.1 **HAIR WASHING**

Hair washing is a common salon procedure. It cleans the hair and scalp by removing the dirt, dust, grease and other matter that coats the hair. Hair washing is a necessity when preparing the hair for other hairdressing processes, as too much grease, or other deposit, on the hair can prevent a tint or perm from being effective.

Hair washing (a)

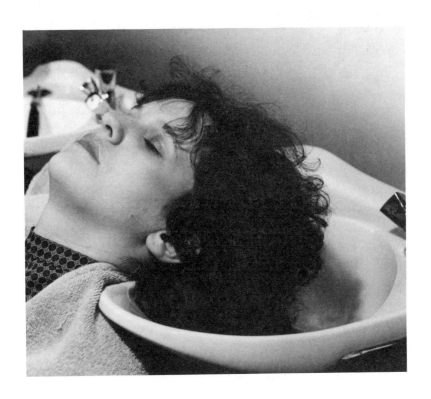

Hair washing (b)

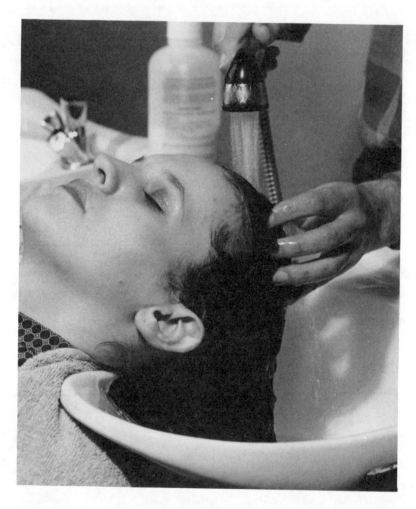

Hair washing (c)

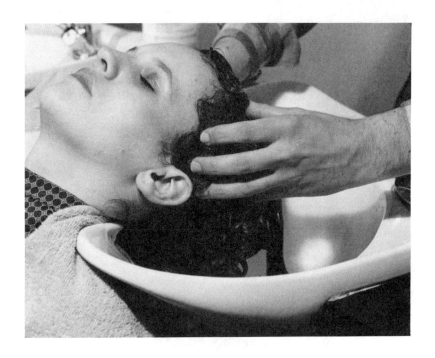

Hair washing (d)

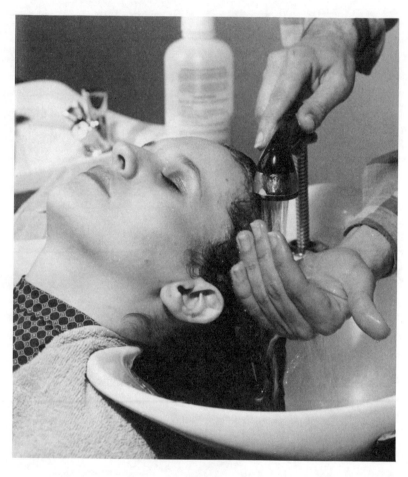

Hair washing (e)

5.2 METHODS OF HAIR WASHING

There are two main methods of hair washing, the forward wash and the back wash. The main difference between these two methods is the position of client and hairdresser and the direction the hand movements take. The position of client and hairdresser affects the way the hand movements are applied to the scalp. The hands should be able to move freely. Too much pressure of the fingers, or harsh and badly applied movements, may result in discomfort and irritation for the client (Figure 5.1).

Fig 5.1   *basin/client/operator positions*

Hair washing, apart from cleaning the hair, directly affects the mood of the client. If discomforted or irritated, the client, on repositioning after washing may prove difficult to satisfy, and this may occur without the client being aware of the cause. Further irritation can be caused by too light or hard application of the hands, varying water temperatures and general carelessness. A good hair wash will soothe and relax the client and make her visit enjoyable. When washing the hair the hands should be firmly but gently applied in a smooth, rotating manner. The fingers should be held in a clawed position and the finger pads alone used to feel the scalp. Fingernails must not be allowed to tear or scratch the skin. Not only is this unpleasant and painful but is also the possible cause of infection. The fingers should not be allowed to tangle or tug the hair; to avoid this the hands should be lifted from the hair periodically. This applies to long hair in particular.

The effect of hair washing is to loosen dirt and dust particles, spread the shampoo and allow it to mix with the water and dirt. Dirt on the scalp consists mainly of grease, due to the natural oil of the skin, and other debris. Part of the shampoo combines with the grease and another part combines with the water. The shampoo surrounds the dirt, combines with water, and is finally rinsed away with more water.

5.3 PROCEDURE

Hair washing procedure follows a generally recognised pattern, varying only with the shampoo used and the equipment available. The following points will help to serve as a guide:

(1) Prepare the hair thoroughly by disentangling, etc.
(2) Run the cold water first.
(3) Mix the hot water into the cold.
(4) Test the water temperature with the back of the hand. Test again after lifting the spray, before applying it to the client's head. Occasionally movement of the spray and water hose frees air bubbles and causes the water to run too hot. Remember sudden shock of too hot or too cold water can be dangerous.
(5) Position the client comfortably. Clean tissue should be placed between the client's skin and the basin. This prevents infection and cushions the coldness of the basin.
(6) After checking the water temperature and the water flow, thoroughly wet the client's hair, always directing the flow away from the client's body.
(7) The shampoo should be applied by placing into the hand; applying directly to the client's hair can be wasteful.
(8) Apply the hands and fingers as described and massage firmly in a steady circular manner, covering the whole scalp, and taking care not to miss any parts of the head.
(9) Rinse the hair and scalp thoroughly and carefully after checking again the temperature and speed of the water flow.
(10) Apply a little more shampoo and massage for a second time.
(11) Finally rinse all traces of lather from the hair and skin.

(12) Turn off the water and return the spray to the correct resting position. Lift the hair from the face, wrap the hair with a towel and gently remove surplus water.

(13) Reposition the client carefully into her seat. If the client is made to rise from the washing position too quickly, dizziness may result; this applies particularly to older clients. Take a little time before allowing the client to move from the washing area.

(14) Finally check that all shampoo, dirt, grease, etc. has been removed from the skin and that the hair is clean.

Moving the client

The hair should now be ready for combing and the processes to follow. When moving the client to another work position do not allow the hair to fall over her face and eyes, as this is both uncomfortable and dangerous.

5.4 HAIR WASHING 'DO'S AND DON'TS'

Remember the following points when carrying out hair washing:

(1) Ensure that towels, gowns, etc. are in place and not too tightly secured.

(2) Use only clean linen and never on another client without first being laundered. Sensible hygiene prevents the spread of infection and safeguards clients' health.

(3) Give your complete attention to the client.

(4) Remove any shampoo from the client's eyes with cool, clean water.

(5) Avoid wetting the client's clothes by directing the water flow away from her when rinsing the hair.

(6) Carefully comb the hair as soon as possible after washing. Use the correct method, without pulling and tugging.

(7) Clear the washing area immediately after use.

(8) Remove all dirty towels, turn off water taps, replace shampoo containers and tidy generally. Make sure the chair is left clean.

(9) Do not allow the water to run continuously between washes as this can quickly empty the water tank. Delay, waste and higher costs can be prevented by turning the water off when not in use.

(10) Finally, do not allow shampoo to remain on the hands. Always rinse them thoroughly and pat dry before attending the next client.

5.5 THE WATER SUPPLY

This needs to be constant for hair washing, as approximately 10-20 litres are required for each wash. The kind of water available varies locally – it may be hard or soft. Hard water forms a scum when mixed with soap or soap shampoos.

Rainwater falls on different rock and ground and chemicals in the ground cause some water to be hard. The minerals in hard water are collected from the ground through which it passes on its way to the reservoir. Water from rivers and streams, particularly in rocky areas, is likely to be hard. The commonest form of hard water is 'temporary' hard water: this contains chemicals that can be removed by boiling or by chemical means. Water that contains chemicals which cannot be removed by boiling is known as 'permanently' hard water and can only be softened by special water softening processes. Water that does not form a scum deposit with soap is called 'soft' water, e.g. rain or distilled water.

5.6 TYPES OF SHAMPOO

Shampoo types are many and varied. The first type of shampoo used was probably water. Water from lakes, rivers and seas is still used in parts of the world for washing hair, clothes and the body. A variety of additional substances have been used in the course of time, e.g. spirit, soap, and now the modern soapless detergent.

Generally, shampoos are divided into two categories: the 'wet' and 'dry' shampoos. The *wet shampoo* refers to any shampoo that uses water to wet or rinse the hair. All kinds of soap and soap shampoo have been used. Soft and hard soaps in various colours have had their day. Green soft soap was probably one of the commonest materials from which shampoo has been made. This type of shampoo, still available, should be used in soft or softened water since in hard water a scum will be deposited on the hair and skin. Scum can be removed by rinsing the hair with vinegar or lemon juice. Rinses can be made in the following way: either (a) the juice of two lemons added to a litre of water, or (b) 56ml of vinegar added to 250ml of water. Water is now generally too hard for soft soap shampoos to be used without special rinses being applied to the hair after washing.

Soapless shampoos are effective in hard and soft water without the formation of scum deposits. The efficiency of these materials require little to be used and must be thoroughly rinsed from the hair.

5.7 VARIATIONS OF SHAMPOOS

Different shampoos are made to suit different types of hair. This applies both to soap and soapless shampoos. Types used depend to some extent on what is fashionable. Whatever form the shampoo takes, the ingredients and purpose of the shampoo to deal with certain types of hair and its condition, are important. A shampoo is often named after an ingredient contained in it. This gives rise to a large number of shampoos with different names and varying effects.

Dry shampoos are of two kinds: liquid spirit and dry shampoo powder. The liquid spirit type is sprinkled on to the hair, massaged and then removed by rubbing with a towel. No water is normally added or used. Dry shampoo powder is sprinkled on to the hair where it mixes with the grease and dirt and is then removed by brushing. This is useful when clients are confined to bed and washing is difficult. Dry shampoos are not as extensively used as wet types.

5.8 CHOICE OF SHAMPOO

This is determined by: (a) the type, texture and condition of the hair, (b) the type of water used in the salon, (c) what is required to be done and (d) what is to happen to the hair after washing.

The *texture* of hair means its quality. Fine hair usually lacks body and is easily damaged. Shampoos which fluff this type of hair are best avoided. Fine, lank, greasy hair requires a shampoo which will have a slight drying effect, but coarse, dry hair benefits from shampoos which contain oil to make it more supple. Some shampoos benefit both coarse and fine hair. Excessive dryness or greasiness indicates that the advice of a doctor should be sought, rather than relying on the properties of a shampoo.

The *type of water* available in the salon determines the types of shampoo used. Where water is hard, the range of soap and similar material shampoos should not be used without rinses being applied afterwards. If this is not done the hair will be difficult to manage. Where the water is soft most shampoos can be used.

What is required of the shampoo is important. Whether it is to clean, degrease, remove lacquer, colour, or treat a condition, the purpose must be considered each time a shampoo choice is made. Colour- and lacquer-removing shampoos, or special treatment shampoos must be carefully chosen and should only be used for the purpose intended.

The *treatment of hair after washing* is important too. Hair to be bleached, coloured or permed should not be washed with shampoos that leave deposits of any kind. Some shampoos can affect the resulting colour or tint and some can block the action of perm lotions. Blond hair might be discoloured by several materials found in shampoos, so before the application of any hairdressing process the correct shampoo should be used. The guidance as to the choice of shampoos generally can be found in manufacturers' instruction leaflets, various product advice booklets, and several books to be found in the libraries.

5.9 PRECAUTIONS

Before washing examine the scalp and the hair, consider what is to be done and the process to follow. If there are any spots, inflamed areas or tender parts present, the manager should be informed, who may then advise the client to visit a doctor. No shampoo, treatment or hairdressing process should be applied if there are any signs of disease present or any doubtful condition. After these points have been considered the shampoo choice can be made.

During the wash make sure the client is comfortable at all times. The massage movements, water temperature and client positions are important to the success of the process. Clean linen and hygienic facilities are most important for the health of the client and enjoyment of the whole operation.

After washing the hairdresser's, or shampooer's, hands must be thoroughly rinsed. Heads may be washed several times a week but the hands are subjected to the washing process many times a day. This can cause the skin of the hands to become dry, cracked and roughened. To avoid this make sure the hands are rinsed each time, gently patted dry, and a little oil or cream applied. Suitable barrier creams help to prevent the harsh effects of washing when used as recommended. Care for the hands is essential if worry and discomfort are to be avoided.

EXERCISES

1 What is hair washing and what does it do?
2 Describe the position and action of the hands when washing the hair.
3 What are the dangers and precautions to be taken into consideration when hair washing?
4 Why is the client sometimes irritated when having hair washed?
5 Why should hot water not be allowed to run continuously?
6 How does hard water affect soap shampoos?
7 How is a suitable shampoo chosen?
8 State which shampoos should not be used before perming or tinting.
9 Why should hair be shampooed before setting?
10 State how water should be sprayed on to the head when rinsing the hair.

PERMING

6.1 PERMING

This is the name commonly used to describe the process of permanently waving or curling the hair. It is used in the salon to describe all kinds of permanent waving systems. The artificial curl or wave in the hair remains there 'permanently' until it is cut off or grows out. If the hair is not cut the 'perm' will grow gradually further away from the scalp until the hair reaches the end of its growing period and falls out.

The perming process involves winding the hair, by one method or another, around a curler, and learning to perm requires understanding of and practice in the different ways of sectioning and winding the hair. The hair is then softened by the application of chemicals or heat, and takes the shape of the curler. Since the structure of the hair is being acted upon, care and understanding of the perming techniques involved must be exercised.

6.2 SECTIONING

This means the dividing of the hair into tidy and controllable portions, which enables the work to proceed with the minimum inconvenience to the client, the process and the hairdresser. Sectioning the hair for combing, cutting, colouring or bleaching should always be carried out for each particular process, and is dealt with in the relevant chapter.

6.3 SECTIONING FOR PERMING

Sectioning for perming enables the hair to be divided into small sections, for ease of working, speed, and to prevent the process from being disrupted. If the hair needs resectioning during the process the perm could be adversely affected.

6.4 COLD PERM SECTIONING

(1) After the hair has been prepared and washed it must be freed of tangles.
(2) Divide the hair centrally from forehead to nape.
(3) Divide the hair from ear to ear over the top part of the head. Hold top hair and sides with clips to prevent interference with further sectioning.
(4) The back hair is divided into three nape and three top back sections.
(5) The two sides are divided from the top front section, approximately at mid-eyebrow level. Nine sections are produced: this is referred to as the nine section method (Figure 6.1).

Fig 6.1 *nine-section method*

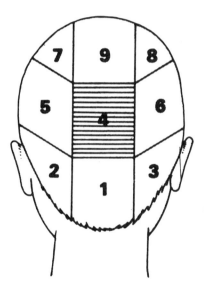

There are many variations of sectioning methods – some produce eight sections, others more, or less. For basic work, practice with the nine section method is convenient. Once this is mastered, it is easier to adapt to other methods.

The tools required for sectioning are: a tailcomb, which is designed to divide the hair; securing clips for the hair; and one of the curlers to be used in the perming process. This may be used to check length and depth of section. Rubber or plastic gloves are necessary to protect the hands. It helps to practise wearing these from the beginning.

Perm manufacturers usually recommend the most suitable sectioning method to use with their products, but all methods must be efficient and precise. Experienced hairdressers divide the hair into four sections; they then take the smaller sections required and wind without any apparent further sectioning. To the untrained eye it appears that sectioning is not being attempted, but in fact it is. Senior assistants know from experience and practice what size sections to take, at which angle, and at which position. Thorough practice with sectioning methods in the early stages of learning will speed working processes later.

6.5 TEPID PERM SECTIONING

This is similar to cold perm sectioning, but the sub-sections for winding need to be double the size. This is necessary so that the heater clamp, which heats the curler, or the heating pad, will fit over the wound hair. The hair section size required for tepid perming is approximately 75mm by 18mm (Figure 6.2).

Fig 6.2 *tepid perm sectioning*

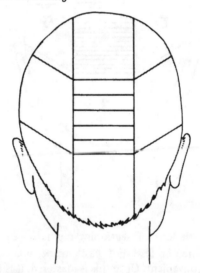

6.6 HOT PERM SECTIONING

The sectioning for hot perming varies and is dependent on the system used. Generally, oblong sections 75mm by 25mm, or 25mm square, are divided all over the head. In the older perm systems where the hair was wound spirally, small square sections were used. With the newer systems larger oblong sections are divided (Figure 6.3).

Fig 6.3 *hot perm sectioning*

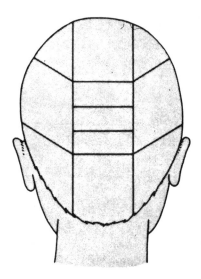

6.7 PRACTICE

It is necessary to practise the various ways in which the hair can be sectioned. To sub-divide the hair into small 'parcels' is, at the beginning, a cumbersome exercise, but proficiency is gained in controlling comb and hair, the technique becomes easier, quicker and neater. Practise at first on a block until the actions begin to speed up. Practise sectioning both wet and dry heads of hair and do not be disappointed if the first attempts at sectioning a live head of hair do not compare with work on blocks. It will take time to become used to the movement of the model, texture, length and hair condition.

6.8 WINDING

Winding is the process of placing the sectioned hair on to suitable shapes or curlers so that the perming action may be carried out. Winding means rolling, turning or curling of the hair on to the curlers.

Method of winding a cold perm curler

(1) A section of hair, no longer nor thicker than the curler used, should be divided.

(2) Cleanly comb the hair, directly and firmly, but not tightly, out from the head.

(3) The hair points should be level with the section centre and placed on the middle of the curler.

(4) The hair points are held and controlled by the finger and thumb, thumb uppermost, of one hand.

(5) With a turning wrist action, the hair points are directed round and under. The aim is to lock them against the main body of hair around the curler.

(6) After the first turn the curler is passed to the opposite hand and turned again. The thumb must not turn too far round or the hair will be pushed away from the curler and fail to lock the hair points.

(7) After two or three turns are completed the hair points should be securely held in position; the curler is then wound down to the head.

When one hand is turning and winding, the other hand should be directing any loose hairs on to the curler. It is important that the thumb is in the uppermost position, particularly when beginning to use this method. If it is held underneath the curler the turning action will be restricted and locking the hair points becomes impossible. This is the aim of practice. To ensure correct winding and curler positioning, in the minimum of time, the following may be used as a guide:

(1) Cleanly comb the hair together to prevent any slipping which will make the winding difficult.

(2) The hair points should be placed on the curler centre to avoid bunching on one side and being loose on the other.

(3) Hold the hair directly out from the head. If it is allowed to slope downwards the curler will not sit centrally on its base section. This causes the curlers to overlap and rest on the skin.

(4) Angle the curler to correspond with the part of the head on which it will rest, before winding, to ensure a neat fit.

(5) Hold the hair firmly without stretching and lock the hair points cleanly at the beginning of the wind. If this is not done the hair will become bent, buckled or fish-hooked.

(6) Keep the curler level as winding proceeds. If it is allowed to wobble from side to side, or up and down, the hair will be wound unevenly and may slip off.

(7) Complete the wind and place the curler in the centre of the section. If it does not fit centrally, rewind.

(8) Secure the curler carefully to prevent loosening. Do not allow the fastener to press into the hair. Hair is softened during the perming process and bad curler fixing could cause hair breakage.

(9) Each hand should be in complete control. This applies particularly when transferring the curler from one hand to the other. Undue rocking or movement may cause the ends to slip, the hair to bunch and the firmness to slacken.

(10) Modern cold perming systems require the hair to be wound firmly and evenly but never stretched. Stretching the hair can cause breakage or frizzing (Figure 6.4).

Fig 6.4 *curler and hair positions*

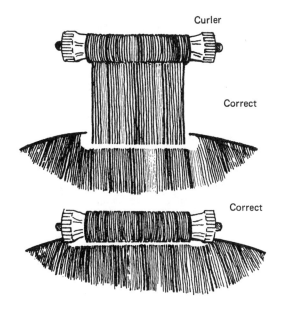

Curler

Correct

Correct

6.9 WINDING AIDS

The *tailcomb* is useful for directing small pieces of hair on to the curler, but the tail should not be allowed to pass around the curler as this may cause the winding to become uneven or small pieces of hair to slip out.

End papers or wraps are specially made winding aids. They ensure hair control if they are neatly folded on to the hair, not bundled up, after combing. The wrap should overlap the ends of the hair and be wound first to prevent fish-hooking. If small pieces of hair are to be wound, half an end paper should be sufficient. A full one could cause unevenness. Only the specially made end papers should be used. Other kinds of tissue or paper may absorb the lotion from the hair and interfere with the processing.

Crêpe hair is an old useful aid for securing the hair points when winding. This allows enough grip for winding and prevents the hair points slipping. Like end papers, only a small amount should be used, or the hair will bunch together.

Curlers used for cold perm systems are many and various. Coloured plastic, wood, bone and china have been used. Different colours are used to indicate size. The bigger the diameter or the fatter the curler, the bigger the wave that will be produced. The smallest are used for winding short nape hair, or for producing tightly curled hair. Most curlers are made with the centres of a smaller diameter than the ends. This enables the thinner hair points to fill the concave part neatly and evenly. This applies particularly to tapered hair, i.e. with hair sections which taper to a point. Clubbed hair, i.e. hair cut bluntly across, should be evenly spread across the curler centre.

6.10 PRACTICE

Practise winding the hair dampened with water, not perming lotion. Dry hair is difficult to wind and it is rarely necessary to do so. It is better to learn to wind the hair in the beginning without end papers or aids. This allows winding and hair control to be mastered. Aids used later will enable the winding process to be speeded up. Practice should be gained on 'live' models as soon as possible, to learn to adapt to the different types of hair.

The first models used for winding practice will in the early stages present problems. Each will be a little different as regards size, hair texture, type and size of curler required, and one may be more sensitive and move about more than another. When a 'blockhead' can be wound in 40-60 minutes progress to live heads can take place.

When working 'live' new techniques need to be developed which will at first slow down the whole operation. The model's head should be gently positioned to allow the hair to be wound comfortably. It is soon learnt that small pieces of hair cannot be wound successfully on the largest curlers; talking to the model when trying to wind the shortest nape hairs does not help; and incorrectly placed towels cause inconvenience. No doubt many other little points and difficulties will be met, tackled and overcome with practice.

The time comes when 'live perming', i.e. using perm lotions on hair, may be considered. The time taken for winding a whole head of hair should then be reduced to about 20-30 minutes.

6.11 ANGLES OF WINDING

Angles should be correct and maintained throughout the whole process of winding. For evenness, the hair should be held out from the head with the points in line with the centre of the section. The curler should not be allowed to 'drop' or be 'dragged', i.e. allowed to fall below the hair section. This applies particularly as winding progresses further up the head. This is a common fault and causes the curler, and the wound hair, to rest on the skin. It may result in sore or broken skin, and possibly infection, if lotion-soaked hair is allowed to do this (Figure 6.5).

Fig 6.5 *wrong curler position on scalp*

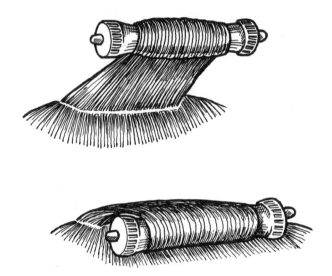

After winding is complete (Figure 6.6) checks should be made for curler position, firmness of wind and any unwound parts. The hair should then be ready for the next part of the perming process – the chemical applications.

6.12 PERMING PREPARATION

As with other processes, preparation is necessary to save a lot of wasted time and inconvenience. The curlers should be separated into their respective sizes, and all tools, winding aids, lotions and other materials should be

Fig 6.6 *a wound head of hair*

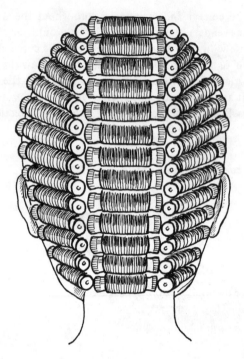

close at hand. This should be done before work starts on the perm. Good preparation allows the fullest attention to be given to both the client and the work to be done.

Remember that the skin of the hands will become softened, like the hair when being permed, the natural oils will dry out, and the skin become sore and tender. In this state the hands could become infected and fine rubber or plastic gloves, or a suitable barrier cream, should be used to protect the skin. Always keep gloves clean, powdered, and do not wear them longer than necessary. If a protective covering is not used at least rinse and dry the hands after using the perm lotion. The application of hand cream or oil will help.

6.13 PERMING

The common factor in all methods of perming is that the hair is softened, made to take the shape it is wound on, allowed to cool or harden, and then brought back to its natural state.

The application of a cold permanent wave is a process which does not use heat. Before the invention of the cold wave system heat was used in nearly all perming. Cold perming consists of the following: preparation of the hair which includes shampooing, sectioning and winding; application of lotions; processing, normalising and finally rinsing. Washing the hair before the perm removes any material likely to prevent the lotions from penetrating evenly. Any coating left on the hair could affect the perming process. Combing and brushing should be minimised to prevent scratching the scalp. The skin must be free of abrasions and disease; if perm lotions are used on sore or infected skin, the condition may be made worse. When working 'live' it is important that all the points made regarding sectioning and winding are applied.

Perm lotions are made for a variety of hair textures, e.g. bleached, tinted or porous. These may be applied using special applicators, sponges or brushes. This should be done carefully to avoid touching the scalp. Lotions should not be applied closer than 12mm from the skin. Instructions from the lotion manufacturers should be checked for the correct usage. Some lotions may be applied before winding, and others may be applied after.

6.14 PROCESSING

This begins after the winding is complete and the lotion has been applied. Timing of processing varies with individual hair, waving systems, salon temperature, winding method and hair texture. During the processing stage the hair expands, the cuticle lifts allowing the lotion to pass through, and the activation of the chemicals takes place.

Hair of coarse and dry texture will usually absorb lotions and process quickly. Fine, greasy hair can be more stubborn or resistant, and the smooth cuticle could stop or delay the lotion entering the hair. Normally, fine hair processes more quickly than coarse hair. Bleached or tinted hair, or hair previously treated with chemicals, will often absorb lotions quickly. The altered state of the hair surface readily allows the lotion through to the main part of the hair where most of the chemical change takes place. Because of the speed of absorption care must be taken when timing and processing hair in this condition. Again, the perm maker's guide should be followed.

Salon temperatures have a marked effect on processing and timing. A cold salon will slow the process and a hot one speed it up. The heat of a client's head is sufficient to start most lotions working. Despite the process being called a cold perm, some systems now require some heat to be applied, which usually comes from a dryer or accelerator. It is usual to cover the head with a paper or plastic cap when applying heat. If this is not done the lotion may evaporate before the process is complete.

After winding avoid padding the curlers with cotton wool. The heat of the head will activate any lotion absorbed by the cotton and if this comes into contact with the skin redness and soreness may result. Wrapping the wound hair in a towel might also absorb the lotion and affect both the perm and the skin.

6.15 NORMALISING

In the salon this is referred to as 'neutralising' and is the stage of perming which stops the chemical action. For this, special normalisers are used. Thorough rinsing is required before the application of the normaliser and then the hair must be carefully dabbed to absorb any excess water which might dilute it. Normalising should be carried out without disturbing the hair, and remain on the hair for 5-10 minutes, depending on the perm used. When the process is complete the curlers are unwound carefully, without pulling, to avoid straightening the new curl. The hair is finally rinsed and made ready for finishing with blow styling or setting.

The curlers should always be rinsed and dried after use and rubbers should be powdered to prevent them becoming soft. Returning all tools and materials to their respective sections after cleaning saves time and effort when required again.

6.16 PERMING FAULTS

Perm slow to process. Winding loose; curlers too large or too few; wrong lotion used; sections too large; cold salon; lotion absorbed or evaporated from the hair.

Scalp red, sore, tender or broken. Curlers too tight or resting on the skin; cotton wool between curlers, hair pulled too tightly; too much lotion allowed to run on to the scalp.

Straight ends or pieces. Curlers or sections too large; carelessly missed sections; too few curlers.

Fish-hooks. Hair points not wound cleanly; bent or buckled hair points; not spreading the hair when using end papers; winding aids not used correctly.

Hair broken. Winding too tightly; securing the curler too tightly; band cutting into the hair; overprocessing; chemicals on the hair reacting with lotions.

Straight perm. Wrong lotion used; normaliser used instead of lotion; underprocessing; curlers too large for length of hair; incorrect normalising; coating on hair preventing lotion from penetrating; poor washing; use of conditioners or other materials before perming.

Frizz. Lotion too strong; winding too tight, curlers too small; overprocessing; processing too long; normaliser not thoroughly applied, or too slowly applied.

Curl or perm weakening or dropping out. Incorrect lotion application; normalising, preparation or timing inaccurate. *Before attempting to correct this fault make sure that the hair is not overpermed.*

Straight parts at sides and nape. Curler angling and placing not correct; curlers too large. *On other parts of the head* – too large sections at wrong angle; careless sectioning and winding; lack of control.

Discoloured hair. Metal tools or containers reacting with lotions used; hair coating reacting with lotions.

6.17 PRECAUTIONS, CHECKS AND TESTS

Before the perm carefully examine the hair and scalp for signs of inflammation or disease, for cuts and for any materials that might be coating the hair. If there are any signs to suggest that there is any abnormality, *do not perm.*

During the perm treat the hair gently. This applies particularly during the softening stage of the process. Do not allow the perm to be unchecked for more than five minutes, unless the instructions for use direct otherwise. Never leave the client unattended when the hair is being processed.

Tests. If it is thought that there may be a coating on the hair, test small cuttings by placing in 20 volume hydrogen peroxide and place further cuttings in the perm lotion intended to be used. This must be done before any application of lotions. If any discoloration of the hair or heating of the liquids occurs, *do not* attempt to proceed with the perm.

Test the hair at regular intervals when processing by partially unwinding curlers on parts of the head. This is to check the wave or curl development. When an S-shaped wave has been formed, without being too loose or too tight, rinse and normalise. The normaliser should be prepared ready for use and applied directly the perm is ready. Delay could cause the hair to be overprocessed.

After the perm check the hair for signs of breakage, and the strength of evenness of the curl or wave. Check the hair condition. If there is anything wrong with the perm do not hurriedly finish in the hope that the client will not notice. She will the next day. Try to correct any fault while the client is still in the salon. At least make arrangements for it to be done, after discussing the problem.

Finish the perm by placing the hair into shape by blow drying, finger drying, setting, or with heat lamps, depending on whether an unpermed or tightly curled effect is required. When dry, the hair should not look obviously newly permed. Naturalness of curl and wave is often the fashion effect required.

EXERCISES

1 What is meant by 'perming'?
2 Describe the preparation of a head of hair for perming.
3 Why is hair sectioned for perming?
4 Describe a method of sectioning.
5 What are the differences between hot, tepid and cold perming?
6 Describe a method of winding a cold perm curler.
7 Why are curlers the shape they are?
8 List three perming faults and their corrections.
9 What precautions should be taken before the application of a perm?
10 Why should a cold perm be normalised?

HAIR STRAIGHTENING

7.1 HAIR STRAIGHTENING

This is the process of reducing curl or wave to make it straighter. Perm systems may be used to produce this effect. Soft curl or wave effects are required by those with straight hair or those with very tight curly hair. Some require their hair to be as straight as possible. The demand for fashion effects varies periodically, but demand remains constant from those with very tight, kinky hair who want it to be smoother and straighter.

Hair straightening

7.2 TEMPORARY STRAIGHTNESS

This can be achieved by most curling methods. Kinky hair may be set on large rollers to produce a straighter effect. Tension will need to be applied to the wet hair which is then dried in position. Heated rollers can be used to produce temporary straight locks, and stroking with hot irons is another method. Neither of these methods is entirely satisfactory since the hair soon reverts back to its kinky state due to the moisture in the air relaxing it.

Hot combs have been commonly used for straightening. These are repeatedly combed through the hair until it looks straighter: a similar effect to that produced by heated rollers and irons. A common result of hot comb straightening treatments is baldness, particularly at the front and sides, due to the hair being dragged, or broken by excessive heat or repeated combing.

7.3 CHEMICAL STRAIGHTENING

Straightening may be achieved by the application of perm lotions and there are specially made straightening creams and lotions that may be used, but the use of too strong a lotion can break the hair. Permanent straightening using perming methods is popular: the hair is first softened, then moved into its new position and finally normalised so the straight effect remains.

Excessive use, and large amounts, of straightening creams or lotions must be avoided or the skin and scalp will become sore and likely to become infected. Avoid the use of metal tools and equipment to prevent discoloration and hair breakage. Negroid hair needs particular care. Although it might appear short, it may be 225mm or more in length, and the tightness will make combing difficult. Always use correct combing techniques and work on small sections at a time. Protective gloves or barrier cream should be used to protect the hands. Vaseline may be applied to the hairline to protect the scalp.

7.4 STRAIGHTENING METHODS

(1) Section the hair into four: centrally from forehead to nape, and from ear to ear.
(2) Subdivide the nape sections into smaller sections. Apply the straightening lotion, taking care to avoid the skin.
(3) As the hair softens, gentle combing with a wide toothed comb may be used to relax the hair. This should then be left combed straight.

(4) Do not continually comb the hair when it is soft, or be too rough with the comb, or the hair will break.

(5) Processing timing will depend on the hair and lotion used. Soft curly hair will soon relax, but tight, kinky hair will take longer. Five to ten minutes is usually sufficient.

(6) A normaliser should be applied as soon as processing is complete.

(7) After final rinsing the hair is then ready for its finished placing by blow styling or setting, etc. The hair retains its straightened shape until it is cut off or falls out.

An alternative straightening method is as follows:

(1) Wind the hair on large perm curlers or setting rollers.

(2) The perm lotion may be applied before or after winding depending on the lotions used.

(3) Process the hair as for cold perming.

(4) When processing is complete apply the normaliser.

(5) Finally, thoroughly rinse the normaliser from the hair after the period of normalising is completed.

(6) Place the hair in shape by blow styling, finger waving or setting.

The result achieved by this method of straightening is a softer larger wave shape, ideal for tightly curled hair. This method is considered to be a safer one since repeated combing is not necessary and the hair is not harshly treated. Make sure when using any chemical straightening product to follow the manufacturer's guide for use.

7.5 RESTRAIGHTENING

This will be necessary as new hair grows. The new hair will appear tightly waved in comparison with the straightened lengths. When the new growth is about 12mm long straightening products may be applied to the regrowth only. If there is overlapping, and the lengths are repeatedly processed, hair breakage and poor hair condition will result.

EXERCISES

1 What is hair straightening?
2 Describe a chemical method of straightening.
3 Why use perming methods for straightening?
4 Why should metal tools not be used in the hair straightening process?
5 What are the dangers of hair straightening processes?
6 How should a regrowth of kinky hair be dealt with?
7 How should the hair condition be cared for after hair straightening?

8 How often should chemical straightening be necessary?
9 Describe the differences between temporary and permanent hair straightening processes.
10 What are the effects of stretching the hair too much?

FINGER WAVING

8.1 FINGER WAVING

Finger waving is a method of moulding the hair into S-shaped movements with the hands, fingers and comb. It is also called water waving or setting. The effects produced are temporary. A finger-waved head of hair was in the past an accepted and popular style or fashion, but now the technique is used as part of a style in training hairdressers and in some competitions and displays. Apart from the effect produced, mastery of the technique achieves the following:

(a) an appreciation of wave shape – the basis of styling
(b) control of hands, comb and hair
(c) exercise for the muscles of hands, arms, back and body
(d) gaining self discipline, so essential for the successful professional hairdresser.

Early finger waving practice should be on a block, but the sooner the work can progress to live heads the sooner the problems of working live will be overcome.

The hair should be clean, well combed and free of tangles. Hair in poor condition should be treated to ease combing and to enable the hair to flow freely for waving. First practise waving at the back, below the crown and parting, before trying to wave the whole head. Hair of medium texture and about 100mm long is best for practice. Slightly wavy hair is easiest, and coarse, lank, or tightly permed hair the most difficult. Waves should be even, shapely and about 30mm in size between crests.

Setting lotions help to bind the hair so that firm shapes can be made. These are now used to assist the waving rather than to retain the shapes produced. Positioning the hair for waving is important. It should be combed cleanly back and if a parting is used, made to lie evenly and at equal angles from the parting. The hair should be returned to this line after each wave shape is complete. This helps the direction and position of the waves. Parting the hair in line with the middle of the eyebrows helps to distribute the hair evenly (Figure 8.1).

Fig 8.1 *position of hair and parting*

Positions of the body, hands, arms, fingers and comb are equally important. Standing correctly - upright with legs slightly apart, and the body level with the part of the head to be work on - will help. The elbow and arm should be held above the hand when placed on the head and only the index finger should be allowed to touch the head. In the beginning this feels awkward but it does achieve control. Hold the comb correctly and comb gently. Do not allow the arm to drop when waving. This will result in loss of control, which is important to the waving process. A comb with both close and widely spaced teeth is the most suitable for waving.

8.2 FINGER WAVING METHOD

The following should serve as a guide:
  (1) Place the index finger on the head. This determines the position and direction of the wave crest. Make sure that the arm and hand are above the finger level. Do not allow the hand to rest on the head. The index finger also determines the size of the wave - the distance between two crests - and hair control.

(2) Hold the comb correctly and place the coarse end close to and level with the index finger. Comb through only when the hair is firmly held by the index finger.

(3) Moving directly to the left or right, without turning and twisting, comb and form the first part of the crest.

(4) When the first part of the crest is formed place the second finger where the index finger was and place the index finger directly under the crest.

(5) Comb the hair cleanly, with the crest firmly held. Use first the coarse end of the comb and then the fine. At the same time position the hair for the next part of the crest formation, again without twisting or turning the comb.

(6) To continue the crest, place the index finger above the line of the crest already formed. Comb the hair at the same angle as when forming the first part. This angle is clearly visible if the finger is placed above, not in line with, the formed crest.

(7) These movements are repeated, and the crest continued across the head, until one long crest is formed.

(8) The second crest is started, to complete one full wave, by placing the index finger below the first crest. Repeat the combing action but in the opposite direction. If the first crest was formed by combing to the right, then the second is formed by combing to the left.

(9) This is continued across the head where the third crest may be commenced. This may be followed by more crests until the nape is reached. The waving proceeds from side to side, gradually getting lower.

(10) When smooth, even waves can be formed in practice, without breaks between the crests, then attempts should be made to completely wave a full head of hair (Figures 8.2(a)-(c) and 8.3).

Full head waving should start about 75mm from the front hairline, at the parting side. The finger should be placed at right angles to the parting and the crest gradually curved round to the front. If there is no parting, start at the hairline on either side. To enable the waves to circle the head a crest on the small, parting side, is 'lost' by careful placing. Waves should not be deep at the crown or near the parting. Deepest waves should be at the front and back. Shallow waving at the crown helps to position the hair so that the waves of both sides fit together.

Waves should be slightly smaller than those finally required. This allows the hair to spread when dry. Do not use clips, grips or wave claws to hold the waves. These usually distort and encourage slack waving. Sufficient control should be exercised to be able to hold waves in position without hair-holding aids. The waving is completed by one or two rows of curls

94

Fig 8.2(a)–(c) *finger-waving method*

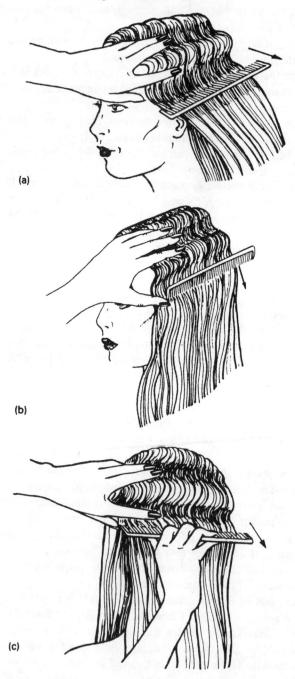

(a)

(b)

(c)

Fig 8.3 *crest formed – section*

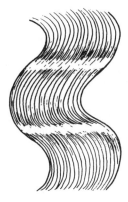

placed beneath the lowest crest. These should fit the waves and form a V-shape.

When dressing the hair the wave positions are retained. They are not usually brushed. Loosen the curls and place the wide-toothed end of the comb between the two lowest crests and comb through to the ends. Repeat this between the higher crests. Support the crests above the comb firmly to prevent dragging. A slight pushing, moulding action with the hand helps to produce full, soft wave shapes. Complete the dressing with the fine end of the comb. Curls may be re-formed over the fingers and a tailcomb. Well-formed waves should retain their shape. *Horizontal waving* is the name given to the method described above. This refers to working from one side of the head to the other (Figure 8.4).

8.3 VERTICAL WAVING

Vertical or 'strip' waving is the name given to another method of finger waving. The waves are formed, from top to bottom, in strips about 50mm wide. The joining up of the strips requires the comb to be angled, to prevent disturbance to the waves already formed. Better control and positioning may be achieved with the horizontal method, particularly at the crown and parting. As with other methods, that which suits the individual most often produces the best result.

8.4 WAVING FAULTS

One of the most common faults when finger waving is pinching or forcing the crest. If the hair is correctly controlled, also the combing angles, forcing should not be necessary, as this distorts the wave. If the hair is

Fig 8.4 *horizontal waving*

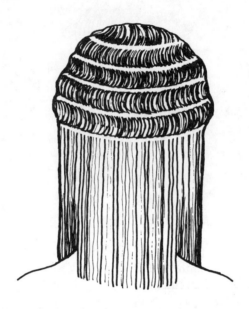

Fig 8.5 *complete finger-waved head – Pompadour*

dried in a forced position the wave soon drops and loses its shape. Allowing the arm to drop and wrapping the hand around the head are other common faults. Control is reduced, waves already formed are disturbed, and repeated effort is necessary. Repositioning the hair after each combing movement is often neglected, causing uneven, ill-shaped waves. If the comb is used to force more hair into the crest to form deep looking waves when wet, the hair will soon fall and look uneven when dry.

Precautions. Use the comb in an upright position without too much pressure. Scratching the scalp in the early stages of learning is frequently done, but must be minimised. Place a net over the waved hair when drying to prevent disturbance. Keep the hair wet, with water or lotion, when waving. Do not attempt deep waves on short hair, a shape that will be retained is sufficient.

8.5 MODERN FINGER WAVING

Modern fashions require fullness rather than a flat look and completely waved heads of hair are now rare, except for practice and period styling. Finger waves may be used in modern styling with good effect, however. The lower back of the head is suitable for a finger wave, preferably at an angle, or a wave or two at each side, with hair swept behind the ears, may be suitable on some. A flat, short finger wave on one side of the front hairline, can be attractive, but there can be no hard and fast rules as to where best to place finger waves since the features of each client differ and require consideration.

The effect of finger waving is similar to other methods of temporary curling or waving and the waves 'drop' as moisture is absorbed by the hair. Lacquers and lotions help to resist the effects of moisture to make the shapes last longer, but the hair will revert back to its original state as soon as it is washed again.

EXERCISES

1　What is finger waving?
2　How should the hair be prepared for finger waving?
3　Describe a method of finger waving.
4　Describe two faults that may occur when finger waving.
5　How does finger waving help in the training of the hairdresser?
6　How is finger waving used in modern styling?
7　What is meant by the term 'joining-up'?
8　Describe how the hands and fingers are used when finger waving.
9　What determines the depth, direction and position when finger waving?
10　What determines the size of a finger wave?

BLOW STYLING

9.1 **BLOW STYLING**

At its simplest blow styling is drying the hair without setting. It is achieved with heat from hand dryers or lamps. Blow shaping, waving, combing or stretching are all techniques of blow styling. The hair is first softened a little with heat, moulded into shape by a variety of movements, and dressed after allowing to cool. The effects last until the hair is washed again or affected by moisture. To get the best from cut and shaped hair it is best to control the drying process; as with other processes, following a basic guide helps progress.

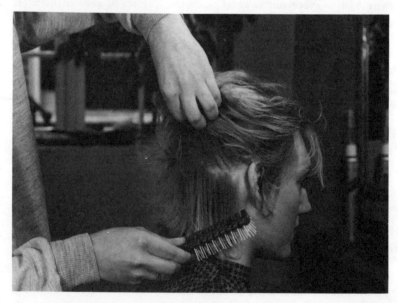

Blow styling (a)

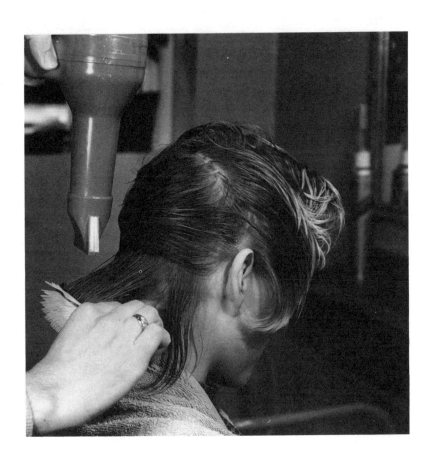

Blow styling (b)

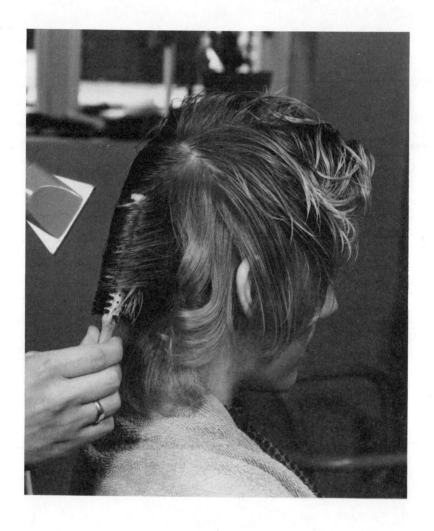

Blow styling (c)

Blow styling (d)

9.2 THE EQUIPMENT

The most important item is a suitable dryer with a variety of speeds and heats. It must be designed to last the long periods of use. Cheap dryers, though perhaps initially attractive, can be unsafe and expensive in the long run. A wide range of dryers is now available to suit most hairdressers. The dryer will need to be light and easy to hold, with controls easily reached, and with a means of placing or fixing when not in use. Various attachments can be bought for the dryer which will help with different techniques.

Heat lamps, hand held or placed on a variety of stands, can be used for drying hair shapes. Again it is preferable to direct the hair when it is being dried.

Brushes are probably the next most important items. A firm, stiff bristle, or plastic, is required. This enables the hair to be gripped, directed and controlled. Soft hair brushes are suitable for finishing only. The half-round plastic brush is suitable for general blow shaping. The larger types are best used on long hair and the smaller on medium and short hair. A range of small roller brushes on which to form hair will be required. It will be necessary to have available a number of different brushes to achieve the variety of shapes needed.

Combs should be professional and heat resistant. Beware when using metal combs as these retain heat and can burn. This applies generally to all tools used; keep all heated materials from contacting the skin. A variety of combs will be required, mainly combs with both wide and narrow spaced teeth.

All tools and equipment should be laid out near to hand. Do not balance hand dryers on the edges of tables, as they may fall and become damaged; place them in safe places in suitable stands or holders.

9.3 PREPARATION FOR BLOW STYLING

Prepare for blow styling as follows:

(1) After cutting and shaping the hair it should be clean and tangle free.
(2) Wash and towel dry the hair.
(3) Apply a suitable blow style lotion to bind the hair, add body and prevent hair becoming flyaway.
(4) The longer the hair the more sectioning is required. Initially divide the hair into sides, back, top, front and nape sections, and then resection as required. Make sure that the hair is placed where it can best be handled.

Blow drying and shaping can commence at any part of the head. On long hair it is best to dry the lower, underneath sections first. It is important that the top, wet sections are not allowed to fall on to the lower sections previously dried; this will spoil work done and waste time.

Producing straight effects on long hair is particularly useful if carried out as follows:

(1) Subsection the hair into about 25mm divisions, and starting in the nape, place the hair on to a rounded, firm bristle brush.

(2) Hold the brush in one hand and, continually turning, lift the hair at the roots.

(3) Always direct the heated air from roots to points to avoid roughing the hair surface.

(4) The hand holding the dryer should follow the hand with the brush. A smooth movement with the brush and dryer, with warm air smoothing the hair, should be continuous and not jerky.

(5) The sections above are treated similarly. Each dried section should fall on to the previously dried section. Do not let the hair fall until it is dry, or repeated drying and loss of shape will result.

(6) The brush should be gently eased through the hair without tugging.

(7) When the hair is dry it may be lightly dressed and finished, but unless the hair is completely dry the shape will soon drop, so patience is required until the hair is dry. It is only towards the completion of the drying process that the shape required begins to be seen.

Practice ensures a continually moving brush, with the lift and control required. Blow styling is best on coarse hair, as very fine hair does not always respond favourably.

When dealing with short hair, care must be taken not to blow it out of line. By keeping the air stream directed in the way the hair is intended to lie this can be avoided. When root lift is required the ends of the hair should be turned and gripped with the brush and the warm air directed into the base. With the brush moving the points around, controlled fullness at the roots can be attained. Short hair may be best formed on to a roller brush, allowed to cool and then dressed.

9.4 BLOW WAVING

A method of waving produced by a comb or brush, well-directed heated air and a series of shaping movements. Hair is positioned for a crest formation and the heated air is directed through a nozzle attachment. The control required is determined by the movements of the comb or brush in relation to the hair position. Repeated combing and drying are required to shape the hair.

9.5 BLOW WAVING METHOD

(1) Start at the front hairline and follow the natural movement.

(2) Using the wide toothed end of the comb a backward, slightly turning, combing movement is made. This is to grip and hold the hair in a wave shape crest.

(3) Direct the warm air on to the trough below the crest.

(4) The air jet angle should be opposite to the direction in which the comb is holding the hair. Use only the half strength flow of air or the hair will be blow away from the comb.

(5) Movements of both hands must be co-ordinated and repeated.

(6) Continually move the dryer along the hair. This serves two purposes: the heat is directed evenly and burning of the scalp is avoided (Figure 9.1).

(7) The second crest is formed similarly to the first.

(8) Always direct the airflow along the line in which the hair is intended to lie. This retains the required line and shape without ruffling.

(9) When the hair is too short to wave, angle, position and dry the hair in line with the waves formed.

(10) Use of the coarse end of the comb allows the heated air to penetrate and speed the process. The fine end may be used for smoothing and finishing.

Do not try to blow wave when the hair is too dry as too much time and heat will be required. When the hair is waved light dressings may be used and a smooth finish may be attained by lightly blowing with the dryer through a net stretched over a frame.

9.6 BLOW COMBING

This is a method of hair shaping with a blow comb, i.e., an electric comb with heated air jets flowing through widely spaced teeth. It is used to dry hair loosely or to produce wave shapes in long hair. It is used by being passing repeatedly through the hair. It may be used to grip the hair, similarly to blow waving, to form waves. Blow combs are designed basically for home use but there are limited salon uses.

9.7 HAIR STRETCHING

A name given to smoothing rather than waving the hair. A brush is placed in, under or on sections of hair, and then turned to grip and slightly stretch the hair. The movement produces soft, slightly lifted shapes on short hair. The hand dryer is used and heated air is directed on to the

Fig 9.1 *blow-waving air jet angle*

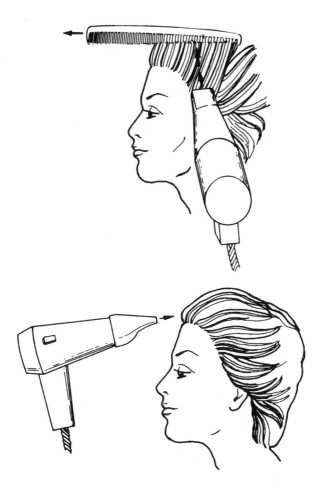

stretched hair. Allow the hair to cool before carefully removing the brush and placing in position.

9.8 GUIDE POINTS

(1) For smoothness and shine always direct the air jet from the roots to the points of the hair.

(2) To produce lift and fullness hold the hair sections at the roots, allow the heat to soften the hair, and remove the comb or brush after allowing the hair to cool.

(3) Use a nozzle to control the air flow. Some dryer attachments include various sizes of nozzles.

(4) Do not start blow drying when the hair is too wet. This costs time and effort, so towel dry first.

(5) Make sure all tools are clean and free from loose hair.

(6) Always check that the dryer is working correctly. First test for use as with all electrical equipment.

(7) Do not allow the air vent at the end of the dryer to become blocked. This can happen if it is held too close to the body when using. A speeded-up sound is first heard and if the dryer is turned quickly fusing might be avoided. In some dryers there is a removable filter which should be cleared regularly.

(8) Keep the dryer nozzle at a safe distance from the head. Burns and dry hair can then be avoided.

(9) Use a cool jet to speed the cooling process.

(10) Learn to use the dryer in either hand. This allows similar angles to be produced at both sides.

(11) Allow each section to fall on previously dried sections only when dry and cool.

(12) Finish blow styles with very little dressing to retain the buoyancy that this technique produces.

EXERCISES

1 What is blow styling?
2 What are the tools required for blow styling?
3 How is the hair prepared for blow styling?
4 Describe the action of the dryer, and the direction of the heated air when blow styling.
5 List the dangers and precautions to be taken when blow styling.
6 What are the differences between blow waving, drying and stretching?
7 How long will the effects of blow styling last?
8 How does the hair take its shape when blow dried?
9 Describe a method of blow styling long hair.
10 What is considered the best length and type of hair to blow style?

WAVING WITH IRONS

10.1 WAVING WITH IRONS

In this method of producing waves or curls, heated irons of various shapes are used to soften and form the hair. The effects compare favourably with other heat-moulded techniques, for example heated rollers and blow styling. Although waving with irons is no longer fashionable it remains a good exercise of hand, tool and hair control and methods of iron-waving can be applied to modern styling and fashion. Appreciation of wave shape, and the discipline derived from its practice, are invaluable.

10.2 TOOLS AND EQUIPMENT

Items of equipment needed are: two pairs of waving irons, a suitable heater, a practice weft and a block on which to place the work. The sizes of irons are A, B, C and D: A being the smallest and D being the largest. Sizes B and C are those most commonly used. Two pairs of the same size are required so that one can be heated while the other is being used.

The irons consist of a hollow metal groove and a solid rod which fits neatly into the groove. Electric irons are available which have their own heating elements. These are now used more for curling than waving.

10.3 USE OF IRONS

The technique must be well practised before live work is attempted as unsteady movements do not permit good wave shapes to be formed. Practice will allow the flexibility and control required: the following exercises are designed to help the beginner:

(1) *Holding the irons.* The handles should lie across the palm, diagonally from the base of the index finger. Support is given by the thumb

resting across the handles. First practise holding the irons with the palm uppermost, then facing downwards. Hold in a horizontal position with the elbow held away from the body and level with the irons (Figure 10.1).

Fig 10.1 *holding the irons when closed*

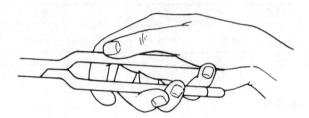

(2) *Opening the irons*. Slip the little finger behind one of the handles and allow the thumb to grip the other handle. After a little practice the irons may be opened and closed comfortably. If the little finger is too short use the next one (Figure 10.2).

Fig 10.2 *opening the irons*

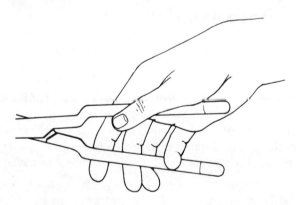

(3) *Turning the irons*. Practice turning the irons in the hand, first one way then the other. Practise pointing the irons in all directions, still turning them. Do not allow the hand to slip.

(4) *Cooling the irons*. Hold one handle and allow the irons to open. Direct the points downwards and swing and spin them. When control is gained very hot irons can be cooled quickly (Figure 10.3).

Fig 10.3 *cooling the irons*

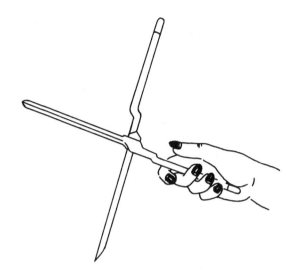

10.4 PREPARATION FOR WAVING

The hair must be clean and dry; greasy hair resists the heat, causing the waves to be uneven, so it is usual to wash and dry the hair before waving. Prepare the heaters and if the electric type set them at the correct temperature. Always test the waving heat by placing a piece of tissue paper between the irons. If the paper does not become charred or discoloured they may be used safely on the hair. Charring, discoloration or smoking of the paper indicates that the irons are too hot and must be cooled before using.

10.5 A METHOD OF WAVING

(1) Comb the hair through and determine the natural fall or movement of the hair.
(2) A section of hair, about 50mm wide by 12mm deep, should be divided. The grooved iron should be placed below the hair section. The edge of the groove nearest the hairdresser should contact the hair section first. If both groove edges are closed on the hair at the same time, two ridged marks will result.
(3) Gently close the irons and roll up towards the head. A tight grip is not necessary (Figure 10.4).

Fig 10.4 *commencing waving – rolling up*

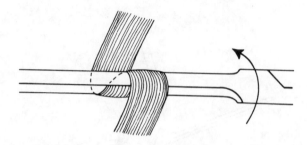

(4) As the irons and the hair are rolled up, the hair should be carefully directed to one side. This must be done gradually or ridges will be produced.

(5) Allow the heat to pass through, and unroll the irons. Then open them and place the groove edge furthest from the hairdresser in contact with the underside of the crest formed. Then gently close and turn under (Figure 10.5).

Fig 10.5 *waving – the turn under*

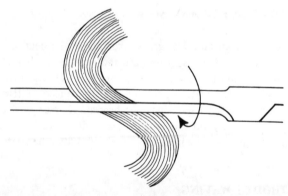

(6) When in this position, the hair and hands should be positioned for the formation of the next crest. Unroll the irons and slide them down to where the second crest is to be formed. The distance the irons slide determines the wave size. About 30mm is an acceptable size (Figure 10.6).

(7) When the irons are in place for the formation of the second crest, roll it up to the previously made crest (Figure 10.7).

(8) It is important to direct the hair left or right when rolling the irons up. If the hair is directed right on the first crest it should be directed left on the second, and so on.

Fig 10.6 *repositioning hair and irons*

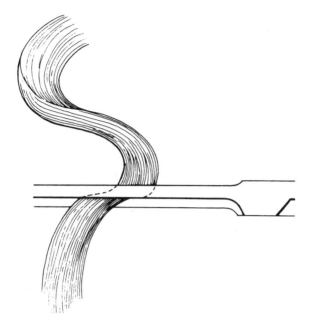

Fig 10.7 *rolling up, second crest*

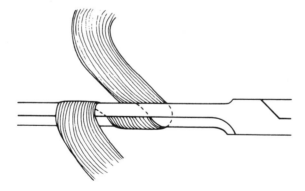

(9) It is essential that the hair, hands, comb, heat and irons are controlled to produce even waves.

(10) Repositioning of hair, hand and comb may be done when the irons are in the under-crest position (Figures 10.6 and 10.9).

Fig 10.8 *finished wave shape*

10.6 JOINING UP WAVES

The joining-up process involves part of the waved hair being used to guide
the shaping of the unwaved hair. Warm, not hot, irons should be used to
do this (Figure 10.10). *Underwaving* is similar to joining up except the top
hair is used as a guide to waving the hair underneath.

The practice hair is best waved in strips lengthwise joining one strip to
the next as waving progresses. Underwaving can follow when the top
sections are complete. Always start waving with warm rather than hot
irons to form the shapes. Hotter irons may be used afterwards to deepen
the waves produced. Hair should be straight to begin with; attempting to
wave crimped hair is pointless. Crimped hair should be wetted, stroked
with warm irons till dry, then waved. Square waves may be produced if
there is little iron control, the hair is incorrectly placed, or the hair is
tightly pulled.

10.7 CURLING WITH IRONS

This process consists of turning and positioning the hair to form a variety
of curl shapes. To produce modern effects the hair is curled, slipped from
the irons, clipped in position, allowed to cool and then dressed. Different
effects are produced by varying heat, tension and shape. The types of
curl formed with the irons are almost as varied as those used in setting.
The ringlet curl is easily formed and so is the roller type.

Fig 10.9 *waving with and without comb*

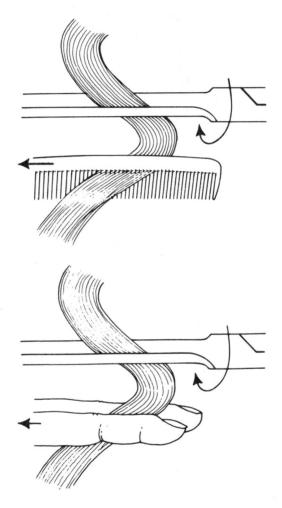

Fig 10.10 *joining up*

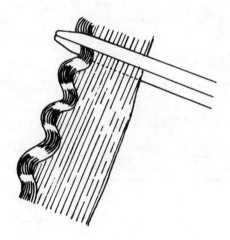

10.8 **CURLING METHOD**

When forming curls, the hair should be held in different parts of the irons for different effects to be produced. The warmest parts of the irons are at the points, the coolest near the pivot. Curls formed at the points are the tightest. Both tight and loose effects can be produced by varying the time the hair is in the irons.

The ringlet curl requires a hair section to be placed between the irons near the root end. The hair is then rolled under and up towards the head, gradually feeding the hair into the irons. By slightly opening the irons on each turn the hair may be slipped from the point end until all the hair is curled. The hair should not be twisted and must be allowed to spiral round the irons. The ringlet should be close to the head with looser hanging points (Figure 10.11). If a looser ringlet is required then the hair may be wound from the points, when it will be tighter at the points and looser at the base.

The barrelspring curl will be formed by rolling the hair from the points in the pivot end of the irons. The root stem which determines the direction of the curl is positioned by turning the irons. As the handles are moved so the directed points position the curl stem (Figures 10.12-10.14).

Short hair should be curled from the points of the irons, which should be slightly opened after one or two turns to form an open centre. As soon as the curl is formed it should be positioned and clipped. Waves may be achieved by reverse curling and dressed when cool.

Waving and curling 'live' present difficulties not met on practice hair. Apart from the forms required, style and suitability must be considered.

Fig 10.11 *curling ringlets*

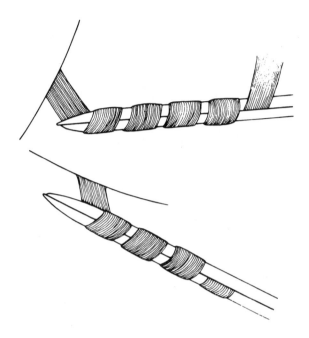

Fig 10.12 *barrelspring curl with irons*

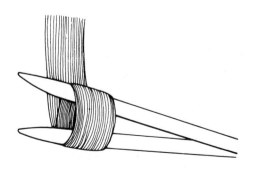

Fig 10.13 *root stem direction with irons*

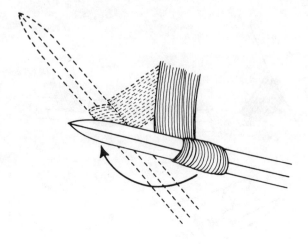

Fig 10.14 *barrelspring curl – slipping the hair*

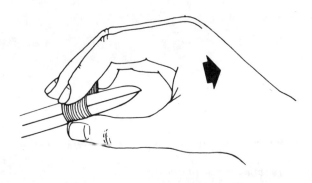

When the student becomes proficient in using the irons it becomes easier to adapt and produce a number of varied effects and techniques. Dressing the hair after iron waving must be done when the hair has cooled. When warm, the hair is still soft and dressing at this stage will cause shape to be lost.

10.9 STYLING WITH IRONS

Modern styling requires a variety of curls, shapes and positions depending on the line of the style. The pattern is designed similarly to wet setting. The difficulty of styling short hair may be overcome by taking hair sections small enough to be gripped by the irons. The larger barrel irons are designed for styling and curling. The roller type curl is easily formed and the open curls for casual effects may be readily produced. Heated rollers are largely replacing tongs for this type of work, but waving with irons is still much used for all sorts of effects.

10.10 DANGERS AND PRECAUTIONS

(1) Heated irons must be tested for temperature before application to prevent burns and ruined hair.
(2) Do not allow heated irons to come in contact with the scalp. A comb placed between irons and head is safer.
(3) After use, heated tools should be allowed to cool before being put away into cupboards. Disconnect all electrical equipment after use.
(4) The use of heated tools on white or blonde hair can result in discoloration, and should be avoided.
(5) Overheating any tool is dangerous and likely to spoil it.
(6) Hold all heated equipment carefully and correctly by the handles. Remember, irons are hottest near the points.
(7) Do not fool around with heated tools. Accidents happen all too easily.
(8) Make sure all equipment, particularly electrical, is in good condition. Unclean or broken equipment can be dangerous, and may hamper the ease of movement required for good results.
(9) Clean equipment before storing. Do not immerse electrical equipment in water for cleaning.

10.11 TREATMENT OF BURNS

Minor burns, without blistering, may be treated by placing under cold water, the application of a suitable burn cream, and covering with a clean dressing. Severe burns should be covered with a clean, dry dressing and the person treated for shock, i.e. kept warm, comfortable and quiet, until a doctor or medical aid arrives. The employer, manager, or senior assistant must always be notified of any accident to client or staff.

10.12 FIRE

If a heating appliance causes a fire, immediately disconnect the electrical supply, apply water, a fire blanket, sand or an extinguisher to the fire. *Never use water on electrical appliances connected to the mains because of the danger of shock.* Uncontrollable fires must be dealt with by the fire brigade who should be informed as soon as possible. In this event escort all clients from the area and sound the alarm or warn others in the salon or area.

EXERCISES

1 What is meant by waving with irons?
2 What are the dangers, and precautions to be taken, when waving with irons.?

Uncontrollable fires

3 How is the size of a wave determined?
4 What happens to the hair when it is waved with irons?
5 Describe a method of waving with irons.
6 How are heated irons tested before using on the hair?
7 How is the hair prepared before waving with irons?
8 What is meant by the term 'underwaving'?
9 How does waving with irons fit into modern styling?
10 Which types of curl may be formed with the irons?

CUTTING

11.1 CUTTING THE HAIR

Cutting the hair to fit the shape of the head is essential to good hairdressing. This forms the basis for all hair shapes and styles. If affects the way the hair falls on the head and, in the final result, all other processes. A well-shaped head of hair will be pleasing to look at and easy to manage.

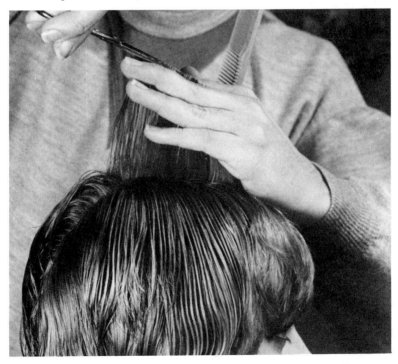

Cutting (a)

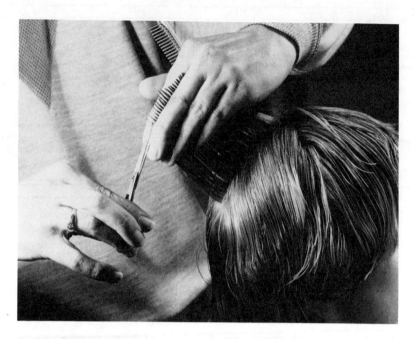

Cutting (b)

11.2 CUTTING TOOLS

These should be clean, sharp and balanced. They should fit the hand and feel comfortable in use. Scissors, thinning scissors, razors or hair shapers, combs and hand or electric clippers are the tools commonly used.

11.3 SCISSORS

Scissors with straight or curved, short or long blades are used. Good scissors are made of special steel, with freely-moving, sharp-edged blades. They should not be too heavy or too long to control easily. A common scissor length for small hands is 150mm, and for the larger hand 175-87mm. Scissors need resharpening occasionally so two pairs, of the same type preferably, are necessary.

Parts of scissors are: the blades, points, heel, shank, rivet or pivot, and the handles (Figure 11.1(a)). Haircutting scissors should be used only for cutting hair. If used on other materials they will be spoilt and become difficult to use.

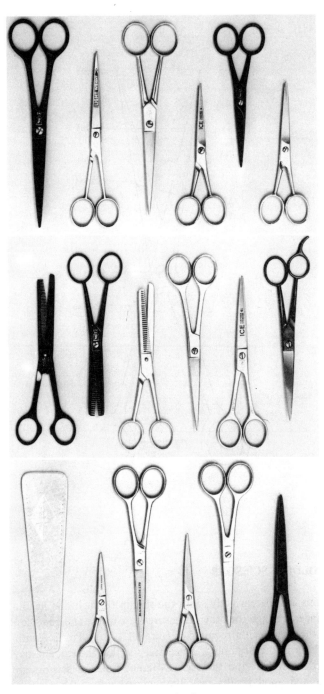

A variety of scissors

Fig 11.1(a) *scissor parts*

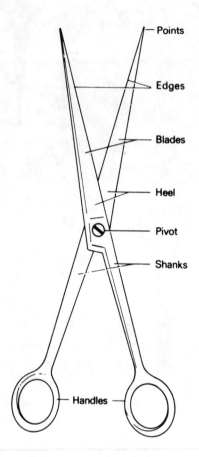

Points

Edges

Blades

Heel

Pivot

Shanks

Handles

11.4 HOLDING SCISSORS

When this is done correctly, with the thumb through one handle and the
third finger through the other, it ensures ease of use and good control, and
allows the movements required (Figure 11.1 (b)). Practice with scissors,
particularly in the beginning, is necessary so that the student may become
used to the weight and the feel. Different types of scissors are equally
popular and good results may be achieved with each type if they are
carefully and correctly used.

Fig 11.1(b) *scissor-hold*

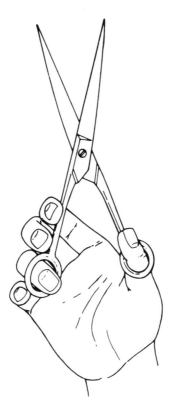

11.5 **SIMPLE EXERCISES**

These will help the hand to move the scissors into the many angles and directions in which they will be used. Practice of the following may be of help:

(1) Hold the scissors correctly and, if held in the right hand, point them to the left. Place one blade on the back of the left hand. Open and close the blades by only allowing the top blade to move. After a while practise this movement without resting the blade on the hand (Figure 11.2(a)).

(2) Practise moving the scissor points into different positions by slowly turning the wrist, first in one direction and then in another. Then practise opening and closing the blades as they are being turned (Figure 11.2 (b)).

(3) Place the scissor handles in the palm of the hand, and with the thumb and index finger grasp them at the pivot and simply turn them, in a closed position, first one way and then another. Occasionally place the finger and thumb into the handles, without using the other hand, and hold the scissors correctly (Figure 11.2(c)).

11.6 OPEN RAZORS

Razors, both solid and hollow-ground bladed, and the modern hair shaper, are commonly used in cutting hair. These tools have very sharp edges and care must be taken when using them (Figure 11.3).

Fig 11.2(a) *scissor exercises*

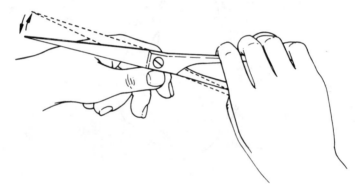

Fig 11.2(b) *wrist action*

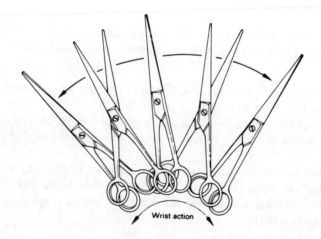

Wrist action

Fig 11.2(c)

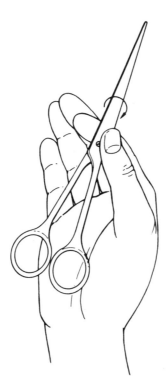

Razor parts are: the blade, edge, point, heel, back, tang and handle (Figure 11.4). The handle is used as a cover for the blade edge, but take care that the edge does not protrude through it. The modern hair shaper has a removable blade with a metal guard. Some have handles like open razors, others have a straight, fixed one. The edges of open razors must be kept sharp by honing and stropping, or sent to a specialist for servicing.

11.7 HOLDING A RAZOR

The handle is opened and the thumb and index finger hold the back of the blade between the heel and the handle. The two middle fingers rest on the back, and the little finger rests on the tang, on the other side of the handle. This hold enables the razor to be moved in different directions without restriction. The razor may be held straight, like a hair shaper, for some movements (Figure 11.5(a)).

The hair shaper has a replaceable guarded blade, with a fixed or movable handle. These are safe in use and do not need sharpening since there are

Fig 11.3 *razor types, and hair shaper*

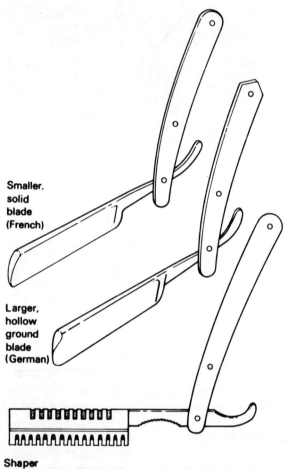

Smaller, solid blade (French)

Larger, hollow ground blade (German)

Shaper

Fig 11.4 *razor parts*

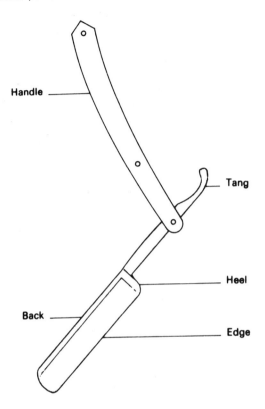

Handle

Tang

Heel

Back

Edge

replacement blades. The guard may restrict some razoring movements but with practice this may be overcome. The shaper is held similarly to a razor but is used with shorter, stroking movements (Figure 11.5(b)).

11.8 THINNING SCISSORS

These scissors have one or both blades serrated and are used with opening and closing movements to remove part of a hair section. They cannot be used in a slithering action as with ordinary scissors. Thinning scissors, if carefully handled, are useful, but have a restricted use. They are held similarly to scissors (Figure 11.6).

11.9 CLIPPERS

Both hand and electric clippers have a restricted use in the salon. They consist of two blades with sharp-edged teeth, one blade remaining fixed

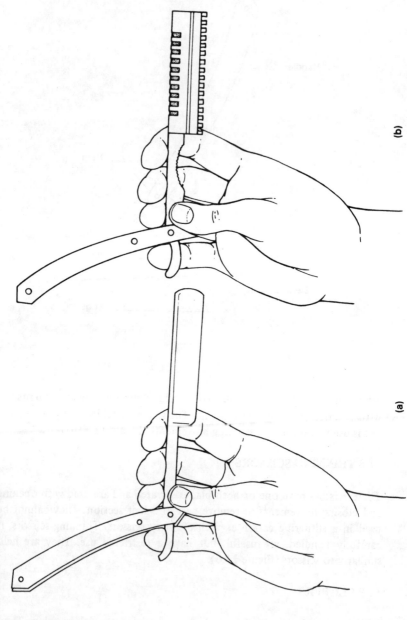

Fig 11.5 *razor and shaper holds*

(a)

(b)

Fig 11.6 *thinning scissors*

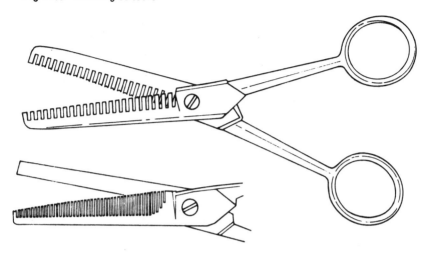

while the other moves across it. The handles of *hand clippers* are moved together to slide the blades. The distance between the blade points, and the blade teeth spacing, determines the closeness of the hair cut (Figure 11.7(a)).

Electric clippers are based on similar principles, but the moving blade is operated by an electric motor in the body of the clipper. When switched on, the blade constantly moves across the base blade. Adjusting screws alter the length of hair cut. The clippers are simply used by placing in position and directing as required. There are several types made, sometimes called electric scissors as the action of the clipper head, or blades, is similar to the effect of several pairs of scissors being operated at the same time. (Figure 11.7(b)).

11.10 COMBS

The best combs to use for cutting are thin, pliable and with both fine and coarse teeth. The fine teeth allow the hair to be controlled and cut closely and the coarse teeth allow for repeated combing and positioning the hair. A variety of suitable combs are made and the choice of which to use is an individual one. The comb should be comfortable in use and easily positioned in the various parts of the head.

Holding the comb is dependent on the cutting technique being used. For cutting over the comb, one end is held between the index finger and thumb – the finger on the teeth edge and the thumb on the back of the comb. As the comb is turned, so the finger and thumb grasp the back of

Fig 11.7(a) and (b) *Hand clippers. Electric clippers*

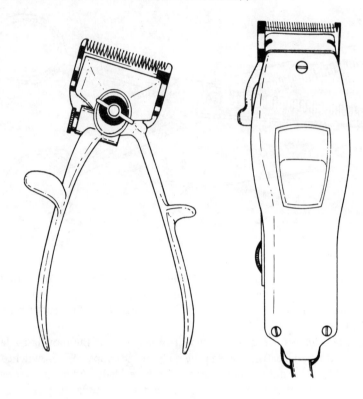

the comb. Simply holding and turning the comb serves as a useful exercise (Figure 11.8(a) and (b)). When sectioning, the comb is held centrally with the thumb on one side and the fingers around the other. For normal combing and disentangling use as described earlier (Figure 11.8(c)).

11.11 CUTTING AIDS

Cutting aids such as gowns, paper strips, towels and capes may be used to collect the cut hair. A long, soft-bristle brush should be used to clear hairs from the face and skin. Powder, lightly sprayed, is useful, particularly if the skin is hot and sticky, to loosen and free hairs on the skin (Figure 11.9).

11.12 CLEANING TOOLS

All tools should be cleared of loose hairs after use. Spirit can be used to remove grease from metal tools and special oil may be used to lubricate and disinfect. Metal tools should then be placed in a dry sterilising cabinet until required for use. Some liquid disinfectants may blunt and corrode metal tools if left immersed too long - always check manufacturers' advice before using sterilising liquids or cabinets. Do not allow these tools to become rusted by liquids or chemicals but if corrosion occurs light rubbing with emery paper may restore them. Badly marked tools can be corrected by having them serviced. Place metal tools on dry surfaces.

Never use dirty or broken tools. Germs breed in the many corners and are easily spread. Scissors and razors may be easy to clean but clippers are more difficult. Hand clippers can be dismantled for cleaning. It is not advisable to take electric clippers apart, although some clipper heads are removable for cleaning. All servicing and repairs should be carried out by the manufacturers or by qualified electricians. With the range of suitable disinfectants, sterilising oils and cabinets available, cleaning metal tools is now no longer a problem.

11.13 DANGERS AND PRECAUTIONS

(1) Do not place scissors or sharp tools in overall pockets. This is unhygienic and dangerous since they may fall on to feet, stab the body, or become damaged.

(2) Loose, cut hair should be cleared as soon as possible and placed in covered bins. Allowing it to gather on the floor is unsightly, unhygienic and dangerous, since it is easy to slip on it.

(3) Take care when replacing hair shaper blades and when using open razors.

(4) Keep clippers clean and adjusted to prevent the hair being pulled. Never use clippers with broken teeth; these can drag and tear the skin.

(5) Use only sharp tools or the hair will be dragged, split or broken.

(6) Clean tools after use and store them in a safe, dry place.

First aid. If the skin is cut, bathe the wound immediately, apply an antiseptic cream and cover. If the cut is severe, try to stop the bleeding by pinching together. Keep clean to prevent infection. Treat for shock, and seek medical help as soon as possible.

11.14 CUTTING TERMS AND TECHNIQUES

There are a number of names of techniques used, with slight differences of meaning. For accurate understanding and application, a short definition of the most common should serve as a useful guide:

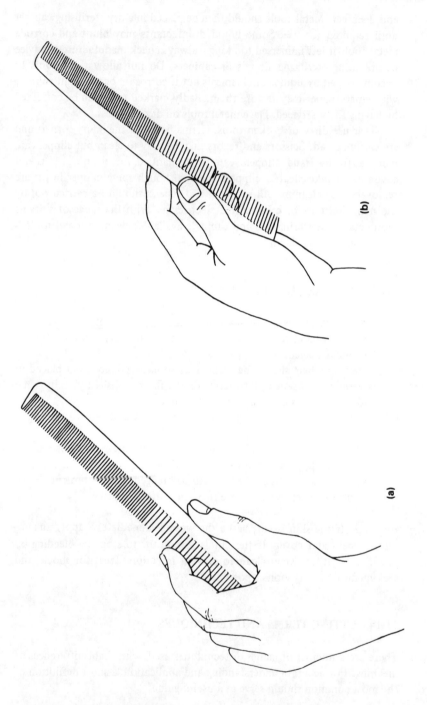

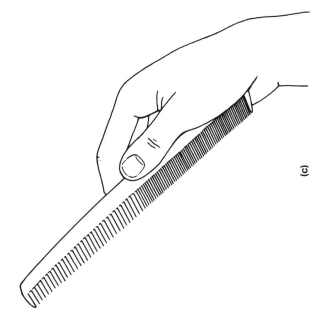

(c)

Fig 11.8(a)–(c) *combs and holds*

134

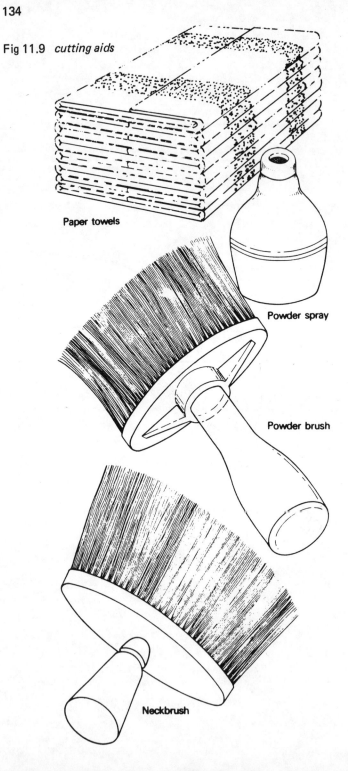

Fig 11.9 *cutting aids*

Paper towels

Powder spray

Powder brush

Neckbrush

(1) *Tapering* means cutting hair to a taper. The technique reduces some hair in a section enabling it to form easily into a point. It may be used to shorten the length of the whole section at the same time.

(2) *Tapering with scissors*, on dry hair, is a slithering, backwards and forwards movement along the hair section. The blades are allowed to open and close slightly. The hair is cut in the crutch of the scissors from the point third of the section, i.e. a third of the length from the points (Figure 11.10).

Fig 11.10 *tapering*

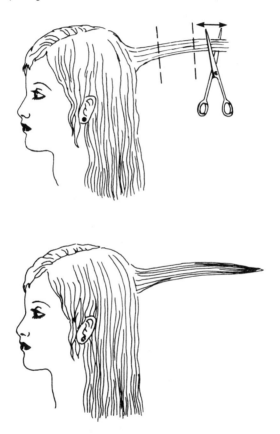

(3) *Razor tapering*, on wet hair, achieves a similar effect. The razor should be placed on, or under, the section at a slight angle to prevent dragging. The hair is cut in a series of slicing actions, backwards and forwards. The razor may be used to shorten as well as taper at the same time. Cutting this way should be restricted to a third of the length from the points of the hair.

(4) *Point tapering* achieves a similar effect by shortening some hairs from the point end of a section. The hair is held at the required angle, and, with a loose wrist action, the scissor points are moved backwards and forwards along the section (Figure 11.11).

Fig 11.11 *point tapering*

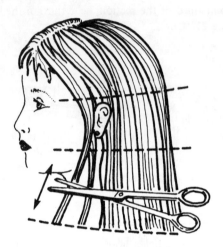

(5) *Feathering* is another name given to tapering. It also describes the effects produced by dressed tapered hair. Like point tapering, this technique can be used to produce feathered effects.

(6) *Backcombing taper* is another tapering method. A section of hair is backcombed, and the point end remaining in the hand is slither tapered. The amount of hair backcombed determines the degree of taper. If a long taper is required then less hair is backcombed. If a little taper is required, a lot of hair is backcombed (Figure 11.12).

11.15 CLUB CUTTING

This is a method of cutting hair straight across bluntly. It is used to reduce the hair and section to one length. The angle at which the scissors cut will affect the positions of the hair points. Club cutting may be used on wet or dry hair. Razors and hair shapers should be used on wet hair only (Figure 11.13).

If a large section of hair is sharply clubbed the resulting line, described by the hair ends, will be irregular. To avoid irregularity it is necessary to cut small sections of hair at a time. Correctly clubbed, the ends should describe a neat straight line, as opposed to a taper where the ends fall to a

Fig 11.12 *backcomb taper*

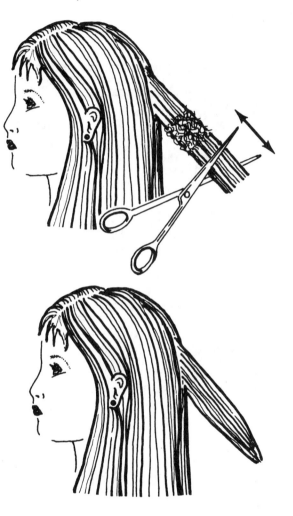

Fig 11.13 *club cutting*

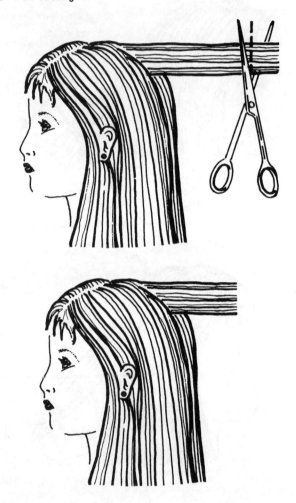

point. Club cutting is commonly used to produce a graduated shape, i.e. hair without steps or divisions, with the hair ends forming an unbroken slope.

Club cutting over a comb may be used for fine graduations, particularly in the nape. This method is commonly used in many men's styles. The hair is lifted with the comb and the protruding hair is club cut. The comb should be correctly held with the points of the teeth directed away from the scalp. If this is not done. a line will result. The degree of the slope or graduation is described by the line in which the comb is moved (Figure 11.14).

Fig 11.14 *clubbing over comb*

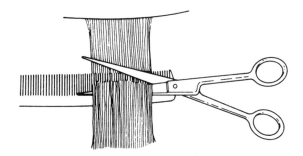

Clipper clubbing is the normal action of hand or electric clippers. These may be used to produce a clubbed graduation in the neck. A section of hair is held in one hand and the clippers used to remove the ends, over the fingers. All clipper cuts involve the use of clipper clubbing techniques (Figures 11.15 and 11.16).

Fig 11.15 *clubbing over fingers*

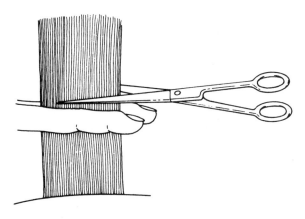

Fig 11.16 *clipper clubbing*

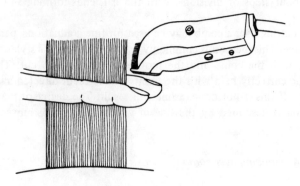

Razor clubbing may be achieved, though this is not commonly seen, by holding hair sections in suitable positions so that the blade edge slices through to produce the blunt, clubbed effect. The hair must be held taut, or the blade will not be able to cut through. The hair should be held firmly between the fingers, and the cut made between the fingers and the head (Figure 11.17).

Fig 11.17 *razor clubbing*

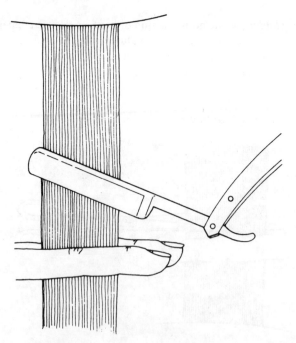

11.16 THINNING

Thinning is a technique whereby the length of some of the hairs in a section is reduced without shortening its overall length. The effect produced is bulk reduction. The thinner section forms a long taper. The hair is cut at the middle third of the section, but if the hair is cut closer than 50mm from the scalp, short, spiky hairs will stick out. This will be seen particularly when combing the hair flat. This effect may be required for particular styles (Figure 11.18).

Fig 11.18 *thinning*

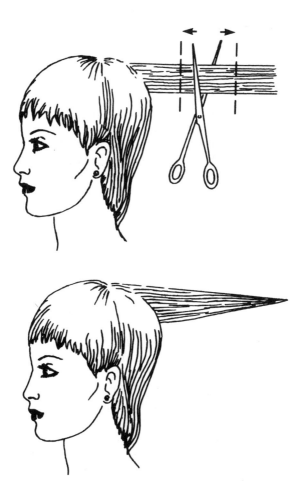

Thinning may be achieved with scissors used in a longer tapering action, for example backcombing, taper or point cutting at the middle third of the section. Thinning scissors with serrated edges may be used. Few cuts should be made with these or too much hair will be removed. The first cut should be made nearest the head and successive cuts should be made progressively nearer to the points. If the blades are not moved along the hair too much will be removed from one place.

The razor or hair shaper may be used to thin hair. Long, sliding movements should be used from mid-lengths to points. Little pressure should be used or the blade will cut through and shorten the hair more than may be required.

Root thinning may be carried out with scissors or razor. Small sections of hair are cut level with the scalp. This is a drastic thinning method used only exceptionally. Some competition shapes may require root thinning, but it is rarely necessary for use in the salon on the average head.

11.17 WET/DRY CUTTING

These are terms used to describe methods of scissor or razor cutting. Scissors may be used on wet or dry hair. The slithering action is used only rarely on wet hair because the blades soon become blunt and control is restricted. Scissor clubbing may be used on wet or dry hair. The razor is commonly used to produce taper, club and thinned effects in wet cutting. Dry cutting should not be done with a razor. The process can be painful, cutting edges are ruined, and the hair torn. Scissors, clippers and thinning scissors are best used on dry hair.

11.18 GRADUATION

Graduation is the difference in the apparent length between the upper and lower parts of a section of hair. It is the slope produced by the ends of the hair when cut at a certain angle. If a section of hair is cut at right angles to the head, i.e. held straight out from the head and cut at right angles to the hair section, the hair will lie evenly on the head when combed flat. Due to the angle of cut and the contour of the head, the ends of the hair will lie neatly on to each other to produce a graduated curve. The term graduation is used to refer to the slope of short to long hair produced in some styles by clubbing (Figure 11.19).

A *graduated cut* is usually produced by clubbing the hair from short at the neck to long at the crown. The nape and back are most commonly graduated in the shortest fashion (Figure 11.20). *Reverse graduation* refers to the graduated line produced by cutting angles opposite to the contours

Fig 11.19 *graduation*

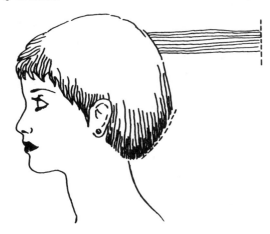

Fig 11.20 *a graduated cut*

of the head. This is used to produce a longer top layer effect where the ends turn under, for example, short or long page boy effects (Figure 11.21).

Angles There are two important angles to consider when carrying out any method of cutting. These are:

(a) the angle at which the hair is held out from the head
(b) the angle at which the cut is made across the hair section.

Fig 11.21 *reverse graduation*

Variations of these two angles will produce a wide variety of effects (Figure 11.22).

Cutting lines are the lines described by the hair ends after cutting. There are two main ones to consider:

(a) the head contour from top to bottom
(b) the head contour from side to side.

Both of these contour lines must be followed throughout any cutting procedure (Figure 11.23).

Fig 11.22 *angles*

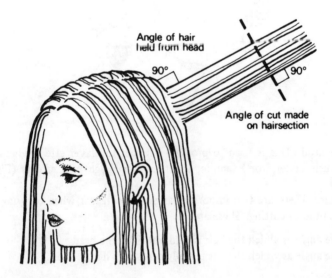

Fig 23 *cutting lines*

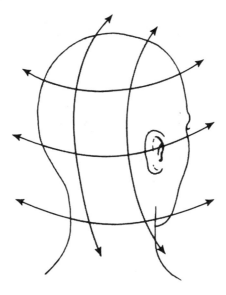

Guides refer to specially prepared sections of hair. These are cut so that both the length and cutting line are determined. These guides should be used and followed throughout the cutting process to produce even and precise results. Cutting haphazardly, without guides, produces peculiar and unwanted effects (Figure 11.24).

Fig 24 *cutting guide*

Cutting haphazardly

R.B. JACKSON

To prepare guide sections the features of the head, for example, the position of the eyes, ears, nose, hairline points, etc. should be carefully followed. Further guides may then be prepared in the neck, sides and front, to be followed throughout the cut. When actually cutting, always use part of the previously cut hair as a guide to the cutting of the next.

The parts of the head to be sectioned for cutting are determined by the contours of the head. If a comb is placed flat on the head the point where the head curves away from it usually marks a dividing line. The back of the head may be subdivided into the top back and the nape. This division is determined by a line passing behind one ear, over the crown and down behind the other ear. The two sides are divided by a line, about mid-eyebrow, intersecting the back line. The top front is divided about 50mm in from the front, joining the two side lines. The crown or top is that area between the top front, sides and back dividing line. It is more convenient to divide the hair into separate parts, for example, the back, two sides, top front and crown, to make the cutting process easier (Figure 11.25).

Cutting practice generally cannot be carried out on practice blocks: the expense would be too much. The practice of tool movements and positions, combing hair at various angles, and hand control, can be accomplished to a certain extent before any cutting starts. Live heads are the best for practice, but care, thought and concentration are essential.

Fig 11.25 *parts of head sectioned for cutting*

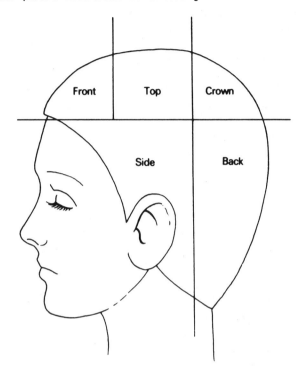

Cutting for the first time can be successful if a simple pattern or method is used. Timing at this stage is important. Speed of cutting can only be achieved after a great deal of practice, but this should never be at the expense of the finally cut shape.

Factors such as the shape and features of the face and head, abnormalities that may be present, or the styling and fashionable effects of cutting, are important. These should be considered, but concentrated on only when cutting becomes proficient. Restrict the number of techniques in the beginning. Later, a number of techniques will be required with each cut shape. Once confidence is gained in producing basic shapes progress to style and fashion becomes easier. The basic cut shapes, with variations, become the means of satisfying a number of clients.

11.19 A BASIC CUT

In a basic cut, this head of hair is shaped into an unbroken line, or lines, which fit the contours of the head. The hair can then be combed, with or without a parting, into any position. It will allow a variety of suitable and practical styles. These should be easy to dress and manage by the client. To this end a basic cut will consist of the removal of excess hair with a variety of tools and techniques available. Although methods of cutting vary the end results should not. Whether the cutting is horizontal, vertical, diagonal, or any combination of these, the hair should fit the head without visible steps, broken curves or lines, unless these effects are required and intentional. The finished cut should not rely on setting, blow styling or dressing for its shape. These techniques should be used merely to enhance the cut.

A good method of cutting should provide a suitable starting point, a clear visible guide for a continuous cutting line, and enable the hair to be easily cut and shaped.

Basic cutting method

(1) The hair, and client or model, should be suitably prepared. The hair must be clean and the client comfortable.
(2) Application of this basic method consists of club cutting the hair dry, or wet, with scissors.
(3) All guide sections should be first cut horizontally and then vertically. All following sections should be cut vertically only.
(4) The first cut made determines the cutting lines and length required.
(5) The first cutting line is determined by combing and holding the centre nape hair down. By using the ears as a guide an imaginary unbroken line can be seen passing 12mm below one ear, through the centre nape, to 12mm below the other ear. The centre of this line is a convenient place to start the cut. Before this is done the hair length which is to remain must be considered.
(6) Basically the hair should not be cut above the nape hairline. The shortest acceptable length may be achieved by cutting the first line just below the nape. A cutting line 50-100mm below the nape line will produce a medium length. If the hair is below this line the hair may be considered to be long.
(7) These are general guides only. For basic cutting, a short to medium length is required. Allowances should be made for a long or short crown and, later, other style features.
(8) Once the hair length, the curve and direction of the cutting line, and the starting point for cutting have been decided, then cutting may commence.
(9) Cutting the nape hair, a section 12-18mm across should be taken. This should be held horizontally between the two fingers resting on the neck. The scissors should club the hair in a slicing, rather than chopping, movement consisting of several small cuts. With this complete, the first part of the cutting line and hair length are determined.

(10) Working on either side of this central cut, a series of further cuts can be made. The cutting should be directed in an unbroken curve from ear to ear.

(11) Having cut the nape hair horizontally, the nape section should then be subdivided and cut vertically. This is done to achieve a degree of graduation and to determine the second cutting line.

(12) Small, vertical nape sections should be combed and held out from the head at a $45°$ angle and the scissor cuts should be made at a $90°$ angle to the section. Each section should be firmly held and overlapped so that the previously cut hair can be seen clearly. This will help to keep the line level. When all the nape hair is cut it may then be used as a guide to cutting the other layers and sections of the back.

(13) The next higher section, about 25mm deep, can then be combed down, subdivided, angled and cut similarly to the nape hair. Each of these sections should be cut vertically only and cutting should progress up the head until the top is reached. The completed back hair should fit the head neatly.

(14) If one length of hair is required throughout the hair sections should be held at right angles from the scalp and the cut is then made at a $145°$ angle to the section. For longer lengths in other parts of the head, the cutting angles should be adjusted accordingly. The line of the scissor cuts should describe the shape outline required.

(15) When cutting the sides, the first section at the side bottom is combed and held down horizontally between the fingers. This is lined up with the cut nape hair, then cut to continue the curve round to the side. This first section is then combed, angled and cut vertically. It should not be held too far away from the head, or too much graduation will be produced. The higher part of the side may then be sectioned and cut vertically. Do not do this without using part of the previously cut hair as a guide.

(16) Cutting the top, crown and front may be done when the back and sides have been cut. The top and crown hair is combed down from a central parting and cut on to the sides and back. Again, small overlapping sections, firmly held and angled, are cut in a continuous line. Work from the top side to the central parting on one side, then progress to the other.

Checking the cut

Having cut most of the hair vertically, check by combing the hair lengths and trim the sections horizontally. By checking the sections opposite to the way they were cut reveals any unevenness and missed hair. Cutting dry hair is more difficult since it is harder to control, particularly if curly or with the remains of a perm. This can be made easier by checking after the wash.

Use a neckbrush to remove the cut hairs. Make sure that protective coverings remain in place throughout the work. Each section should be cleanly combed and angled correctly. When the cut is complete, and checked, the shape may be improved by blow styling, setting, tonging or dressing.

Adaption from the basic shape to simple styles becomes easier once the basic method of cutting is achieved. The cutting lines at the sides may be varied to line up with the chin, mouth, nose, eye or eyebrow. The front hair may be left long, or cut short. Necklines may be cut round, square, pointed or uneven, as required. Each of these may be considered to achieve a varied basic cut, which enables the first style cutting effects to be produced (Figure 11.26).

Fig 11.26 *adapting basic shape*

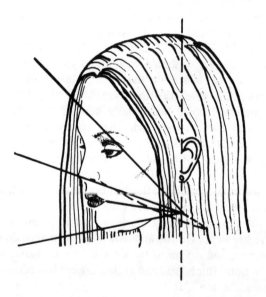

11.20 FASHION CUTTING

Fashion cutting involves cutting hair to a particular shape. This may follow a style line of the past or the present. To achieve the results required a variety of techniques and methods may be used: to create an effect practically 'anything goes'. To create pleasing and unique effects a carefully prepared pattern of cutting should be followed, based on an understanding of hairstyling.

The features of the face and head should be assessed before starting to cut. The general shape of the head, nose, ears, eyes and mouth should be closely looked at and it should be noted whether the facial profile is concave or convex. The lowest point of the chin, in relation to the top, back, and nape, should be examined. Positions of facial features as related to the front hairline should also be noted.

The length, quality, quantity, texture and general state of the hair must be considered; this applies particularly to the effects of the previous cut. Abnormal aspects should be discussed and dealt with. For instance, a large cyst requires a longer length of hair to be left so that it is not made to look obvious. Each of these points is important and may be used as guide to cutting lines and angles for the creation of individual shapes.

The techniques and methods to use are determined by examination of the hair. Some hair may need to be tapered and then lightly clubbed; some may need clubbing; thinning may be required if the hair is thick and bulky. The choice of wet or dry cutting is an individual one determined by experience and the hair to be cut, but it is considered to be more hygienic to wash the hair before cutting.

11.21 CUTTING LINES AND ANGLES

These are achieved by holding the sections of hair away from the head. The positions held and cut determine the positions the sections take when combed on to the head after cutting.

A section of hair held at right angles (90° angle) from the back of the head, and cut at right angles (90° angle) to the hair section, will produce a 45° angle of graduation, that is, the gradient between the top and bottom of the vertical section (Figure 11.27(a)).

A section of hair held at right angles, and cut at a 45° angle, will produce a steeper graduation, which is of use in short nape styles (Figure 11.27(b)).

A section of hair held out vertically at right angles, and cut at a 145° angle, will produce a 'level length', where all the ends of the hair are level without graduation (Figure 11.27(c) and (d)).

For all styles and fashion shapes the line of cutting, i.e. the outline shape produced by combing the hair out from the head, must be adjusted. The angles of cutting will vary with the different lengths required by the shape. As with basic cutting, the first cutting line may be determined in the nape of the neck, as well as determining the length. The second cutting line varies with the different lengths required throughout the shape (Figure 11.28(a) and (b); 11.29(a) and (b)).

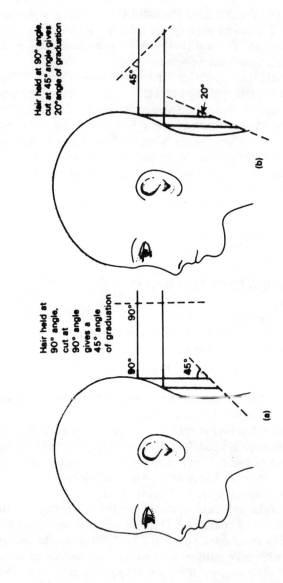

Fig 11.27 (a) – (b) *cutting lines and angles*

Hair held at 90° angle,
cut at
90° angle
gives a
45° angle
of graduation

90°

90°

45°

(a)

Hair held at 90° angle,
cut at 45° angle gives
20° angle of graduation

45°

20°

(b)

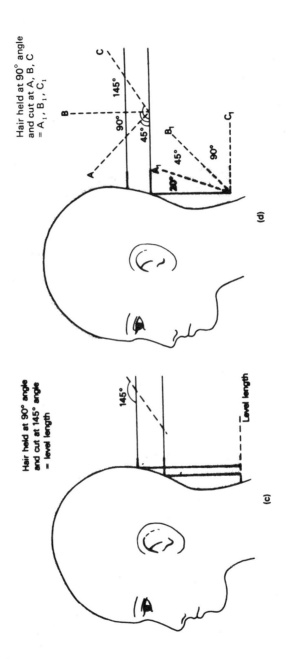

Fig 11.27(c)–(d)

Hair held at 90° angle
and cut at 145° angle
= level length

(c)

Hair held at 90° angle
and cut at A, B, C
= A_1, B_1, C_1

(d)

Fig 11.28(a) and (b) *varied second cutting line – side view*

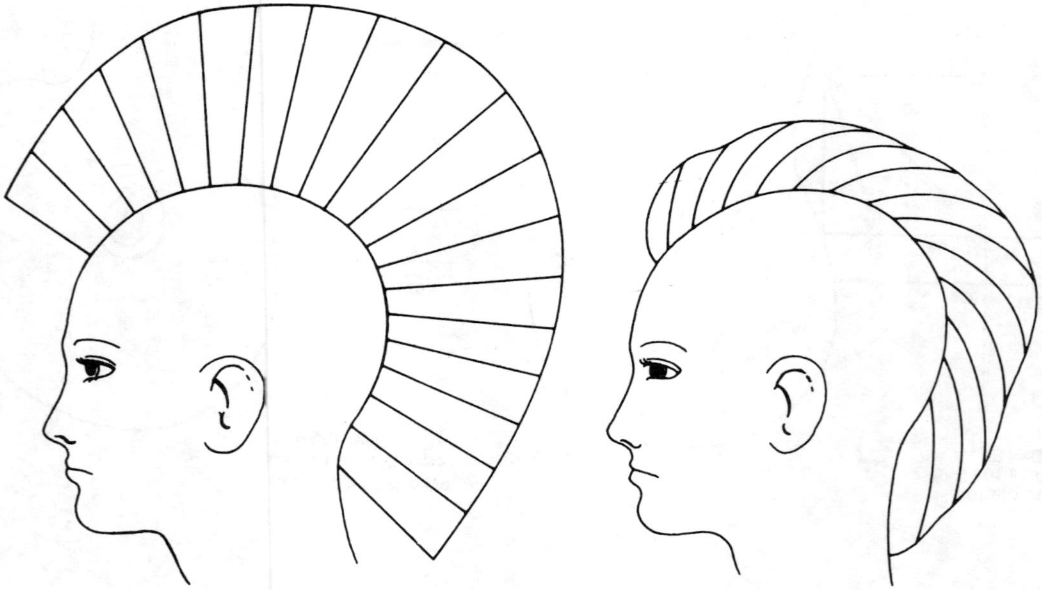

(a)

(b)

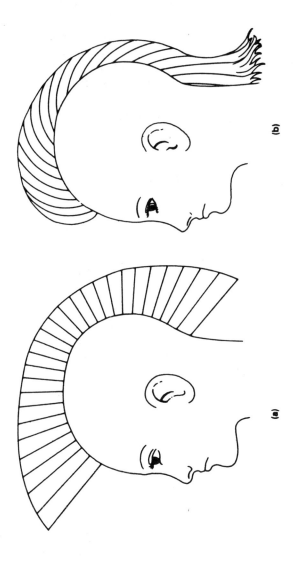

Fig 11.29(a) and (b)   *varied second cutting lines – hair in position*

For side hair cutting, vertical sections may be combed forward towards the face, to vary length or graduation. The hair nearer the face will be cut shorter than the hair towards the back. This can be clearly seen when the hair is combed back into its normal position. This method is required for flicked, wispy side effects in short styles.

The variations of angling hair sections, and the cutting angles, produce a variety of effects. If each of the angle directions are followed from one section to the next, good shapes may be achieved, but if the angles continually vary, section after section, uneven effects are produced. It is important to follow the head contours, and for the cutting lines to describe the outline of the shape and lengths required (Figure 11.30(a) and (b)).

11.22 CUTTING LONG HAIR

To cut long hair so that it falls evenly at the ends is simply achieved by following the basic pattern. Cutting angles may be varied by choosing different guide points. If the hair is fine the clubbing technique is best used. The length, and first cutting line, are determined by cutting, to below each ear, from cheekbone to cheekbone, to the corners of the mouth, or to the point of the chin. Since graduation is not required, and the hair is to fall level, following sections at the back are combed down and cut horizontally, to a point just below the first cut section. This allows for a natural hair lift and will not show graduation. If the hair is to turn under, reverse graduation is achieved by cutting a fraction lower than the first cut section. This produces full, swinging hair, that is, hair, level at the ends, which swings back into position when moved.

If a degree of graduation is required, after preparing the length and cutting line in the nape, the following sections are cut on to it by holding them out and cutting at right angles. The determined length must be followed and the angle of cut carefully executed (Figure 11.31(a)-(d)).

11.23 CUTTING SHORT, CURLY SHAPES

It is best to do this using the tapering technique, since tapered hair holds a curl longer. Prepare the nape hair and cut the length and first cutting line horizontally. The second line, and graduation required, is cut by taking vertical sections. If the hair is held at a 90° angle, and cut at a 90° angle throughout, a short style is produced with a suitable degree of graduation (Figure 11.32).

The sides, depending on whether they are to be dressed forward or back, must be angled and cut accordingly. A fringe, common with short styles, may be cut by combing the hair forward. The length and shape may be determined by tapering. Use parts of the nose, eyes or brows as a guide.

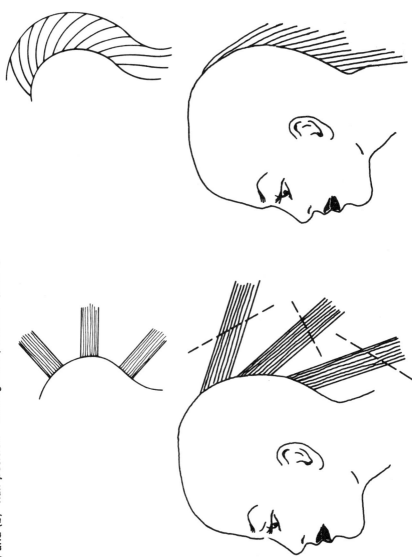

Fig 11.30(a) and (b) *hair position – cutting. Hair position – placing*

158

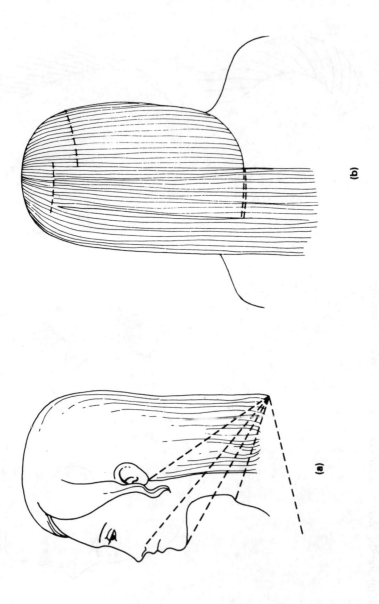

Fig 11.31(a) - (b) *cutting long hair*

(a)

(b)

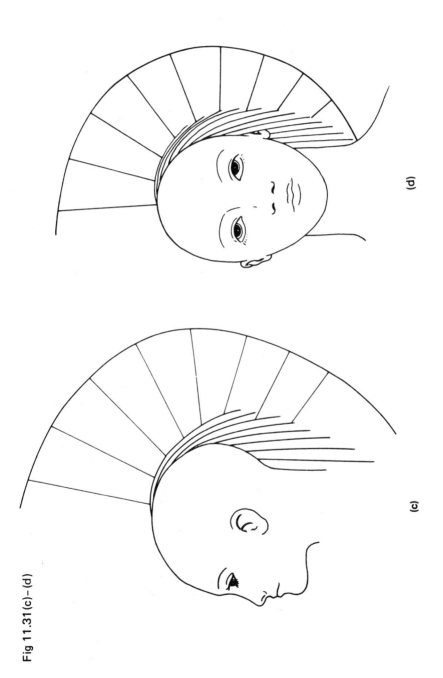

Fig 11.31(c)–(d)

(c)

(d)

Fig 11.32 *cutting short curly shapes*

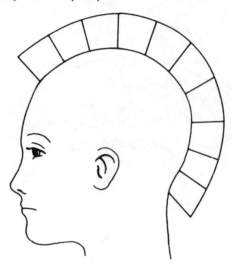

Fringes are cut similarly to nape hair. Directional growth must be considered and allowed for when determining the fringe length. Unless a hard fringe line is required, club cut only when the hair is correctly angled.

11.24 GEOMETRIC CUTTING

This type of cutting is used to produce hard and soft effects by varying the cutting lines at different angles. The shape and line of the head, face, hairlines and other features are used to determine angles of cutting, on which geometric effects are dependent. The shorter shapes are more exacting since they cannot be altered or corrected by dressing. Precise and accurate cutting is essential. It should not be attempted unless the techniques and principles are fully understood (Figure 11.33(a)-(c)).

11.25 CUTTING LONG AND SHORT EFFECTS

Cutting these in the same style, is a popularly effective means of shaping. The hair is usually shortest at the top and back of the head, with the longest lengths at the sides.

The bottom cutting line is determined by choosing a low point. The hair is cut straight or curved, and the angle of graduation sharply inclined towards the neck. The following sections are cut with the same degree of graduation but in the opposite direction. Alternatively, the nape section may be cut with little or no graduation, and the following section sharply graduated.

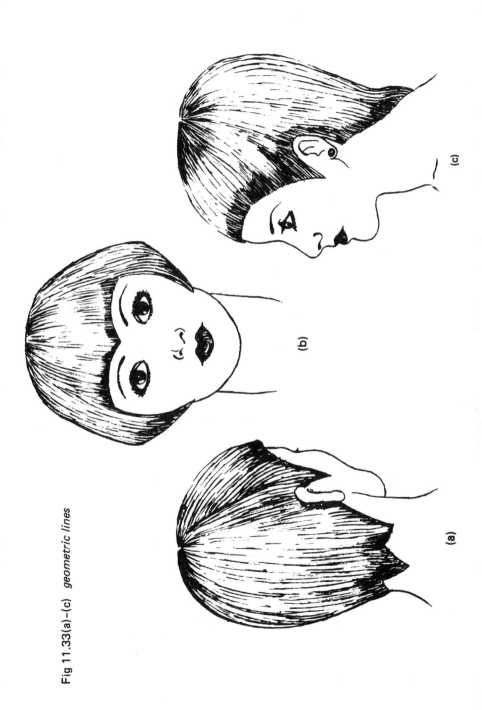

Fig 11.33(a)–(c) *geometric lines*

The cutting line should be sharply angled to the top of the ears and the reverse angle used to shape the sides. This separates the sides from the back. The sides and front may be heavily tapered to produce long, wispy effects. Both tapering and clubbing techniques can be used with scissors or razors for these styles (Figure 11.34).

Shingles, semi-shingles and the Eton crop are some of the names given to short nape styles which were popular between the Wars. The technique involved is similar to that required for cutting men's styles. Clubbing over the comb is the technique used to produce close, sharp graduation in the neck sections. The shingle and Eton crop were graduated high in the neck. The semi-shingle has a softer effect and is graduated lower in the neck (Figure 11.35).

Fig 11.34 *long and short effects*

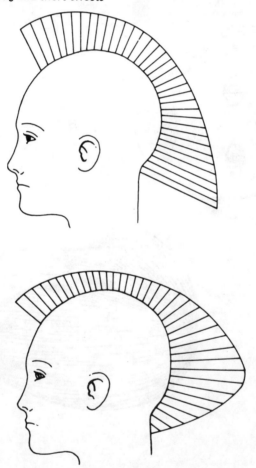

Fig 11.35 *semi-shingle*

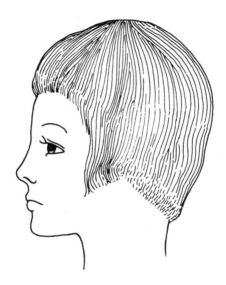

11.26 CUTTING MEN'S HAIR

This differs from cutting ladies' hair in that the shapes worn and face and head shapes vary. Similar techniques are used, but methods of application differ. Cutting short styles requires precision and there is little or no way to disguise mistakes. Clipper cutting was commonly used to produce the 'short back and sides' military fashion, but this was designed more for hygiene than style. Variations of closely cropped styles have been worn over the years. Like other styles it seems that it becomes popular periodically.

Generally, most of the men's styles produced should fit the heads on which they are to be worn. Very short, or skinned heads, are rarely suitable except where certain fashion effects are required. Longer styles for men may be cut similarly to ladies' styles. Feminine effects are as unsuitable on men as masculine shapes are on ladies, but it depends on what is required and what effect is to be achieved. Although there are many similarities, each type of cutting requires skill and experience. No doubt specialisation in one or the other will continue, despite the fact that cutting a head of hair, to fit the male or female head, remains basically the same (Figure 11.36).

Fig 11.36 *men's shapes*

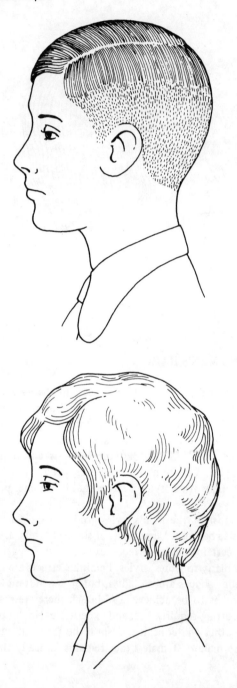

11.27 VARIATIONS OF CUTS

Variations are made to suit individuals and to meet their requirements. Apart from the similarities of cutting methods, different names may be given to each. Bobbing, layer cutting, layering and bevel cutting are the effects produced by tapering and clubbing. The Eton crop, Egyptian bob and cap cut are some of the names given to styles or cuts. A client asking for a named cut must be interpreted correctly. Long, medium and short hair varies with each client. Beware the confusion of names given to styles and what is being requested.

Necklines may be curved, straight, pointed or graduated high or low. The lower the graduation, the softer the style will be and care should be taken when cutting above the natural hairline to avoid harsh effects, unless this is the style effect required. Hair remaining below the hairline may be removed with clippers or scissor points. Steps or lines left in graduated work will spoil the effect; it is better to soften all lines unless stark effects are wanted (Figure 11.37(a)–(c)).

11.28 TRIMMING

Trimming means the removal of small amounts of regrown hair, usually to retain the original cut shape. The same techniques, cutting lines and

Fig 11.37 (a) - (b) *necklines*

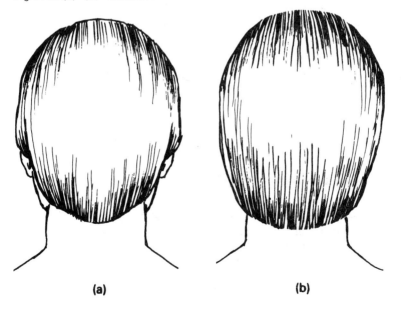

(a)   (b)

Fig 11.37(c)

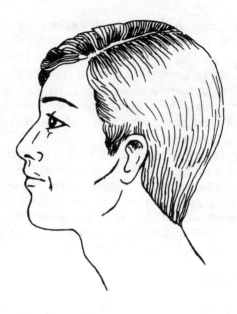

angles, should be used if the shape is to be reproduced. When restyling make sure the hair is long enough to cut the style requested. Note abnormalities, and discuss with the client what is involved. Often a style is requested before the hair is long enough to cut into it. Some styles require certain lengths and it takes time for the hair to grow before they can be achieved. The time and effort given to these considerations will help to achieve the desired effects and avoid any possible misunderstandings.

EXERCISES

1 What is meant by the term 'cutting'?
2 How should scissors be correctly held?
3 Why should scissors be held correctly?
4 Describe suitable scissor exercises.
5 What is achieved by exercising the scissors?
6 How are metal tools cleaned?
7 What precautions should be taken when cutting?
8 What are the techniques of cutting?
9 What are cutting guides, lines and angles?
10 Describe a method of cutting a hair shape.

DRESSING

12.1 DRESSING THE HAIR

Dressing consists of blending shapes from the way the hair was set or placed. The completed shape is called a dressing, coiffure or hair-do. There are several techniques used to blend or bind the hair together.

12.2 DRESSING WITH A BRUSH

The hair is placed into a finished shape with the use of the brush only. The brush should be applied to the ends of the hair and carefully stroked. This is repeated, moving further up the head through the set waves and curls. The brushing action should be gentle but firm and the hair should be moulded into shape. The dressing is finished when the hair has been placed and the 'look' has been achieved.

12.3 BACKBRUSHING

This technique involves the pushing of some hair back so that the main body of the hair stands away from the head. This is used to produce lift or height and to bind the hair together. The amount of hair backbrushed determines the amount of lift or binding. If the hair is tapered a greater lift may be achieved more easily (Figure 12.1).

12.4 A BACKBRUSHING METHOD

This may be applied by holding sections of hair out from the head; for the maximum lift these sections should be held directly out and then angled towards the final position. First the brush edge is placed on top of the section, then with a slight turning action the brush is made to slide some hairs back towards the head - if the movement is too heavy the section

Fig 12.1 *backbrushing*

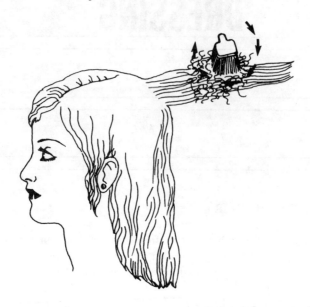

will be pulled from the hand. It is necessary to gradually place the section by directing after each brush stroke. For maximum lift the hair is pushed close to the roots, holding the section at right angles. In some dressings only small amounts of hair need to be pushed back. It is the backbrushed hair that supports the section. This allows the surface of the section to be smoothed and a full, light shape produced. The tangled, pushed-back hair should not be visible on completion (Figure 12.2).

12.5 BACKCOMBING

Backcombing is similar to backbrushing: the comb is used to push back the shorter hairs within the section. This allows the full, high dressed hair to be supported, and the height to be retained. Backcombing is usually used to produce a greater degree of backdressing, as more hair is pushed back than would be achieved with a brush.

12.6 A BACKCOMBING METHOD

(1) Sections of hair are held out directly, or at varying angles, from the head: the angle depends on the dressed position required.
(2) The fine end of the dressing comb is placed on the underside of the section, usually near the roots.

Fig 12.2 *backbrushing – stages*

(3) The comb is gently turned and pushed back towards the head, the shorter hairs are doubled back and bind in with the other hairs.

(4) This action is repeated along the section until the points are reached.

(5) The backcombed section is then pushed away so that following sections may be dealt with similarly.

(6) This continues in those parts of the dressing where binding, lift, fullness or height are required.

After backcombing, the hair may be positioned with the fingers. Finally, the wide end of the comb may be used to smooth the surface. If the hair is backcombed above the section surface smoothing becomes difficult because the backcombing will be dragged out, the comb should not be allowed to penetrate the section too far to avoid dragging and the loss of the effects of the backcombing.

Backdressing, that is, backcombing or backbrushing, may be applied to any part of the hair in any part of the head requiring these effects (Figure 12.3(a)–(c)).

12.7 TEASING

Teasing the hair with a pin, or the tail of a tailcomb, may be used to complete the dressing. By carefully using the pin, or tail, parts of the hair

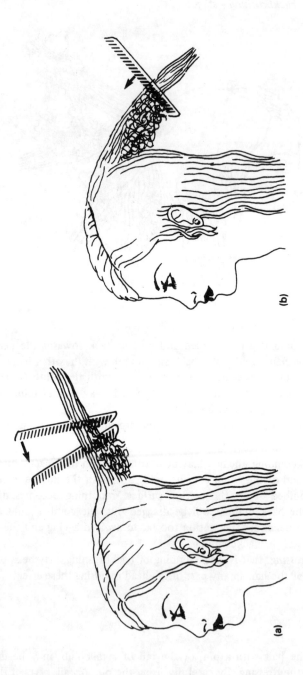

Fig 12.3 (a)–(b) *backcombing – stages*

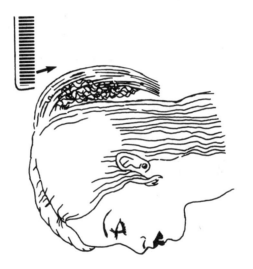

Fig 12.3(c)

may be slightly lifted to achieve balance or to cover an exposed area of backdressing. When dealing with small pieces of hair it is important to use the tips of the fingers or implement, to avoid general disturbance. Hands can be used for finishing the dressing, but they must be used lightly: if they are used to continually pat down the shape then all dressing effects will be lost. The result could be flatter than if no backdressing was used. The hands should be angled so that the palms do not touch the hair or the head when working.

12.8 **MIRRORS**

These are used to check the progress of the work. Carefully watching the lines and movements produced means that time-wasting alterations can be avoided: at the same time other suitable shapes can be seen. Do not look too closely or too long at one part of the head as this can only restrict the overall view: step back so that the whole outline can be seen. The hand mirror is useful for the client to view the finished effects from the sides and back.

12.9 **A SIMPLE DRESSING**

This may be carried out as follows:
(1) Brush the hair firmly, starting at the nape. Gradually work up the head until the front is reached.
(2) When the brush can be freely moved through the hair, brush against the set direction and then finally in the direction intended.
(3) With the set blended, the comb or brush can be used to distribute the hair. It helps at this stage to follow the movements set or placed.
(4) As the hair is positioned, the hand lightly strokes it, and if height is required, gently pushes the hair from the head.

A well placed head of hair may be quickly dressed this way, without backdressing. This may be all that is required by some clients and some styles. The directions in which the hair is set or blow styled determines the variation of movements in the final dressing.

12.10 **STYLE DRESSING**

Style dressing usually requires height and volume and a certain amount of backdressing, but this depends on the style required. Where fullness is needed small sections are taken and backdressed piece by piece where the lift is required. Allowance must be made for blending the areas between full height and flatness; this is achieved by reducing the angle of backdressing for the overall balance. By following the set lines dressing is soon accomplished: if the set has to be corrected by the dressing more time and usually backdressing is required.

12.11 OVERDRESSING

This is one of the commonest faults of dressing. The shape, balance and movements are reduced by continually fiddling with the hair, but by closely watching what one is doing the desired shape is soon recognised. Salon dressing shapes are usually realised long before dressing is complete. The dressing should be planned by deciding what is to be done, where to start and finish, and how it is to be achieved. This depends on the shape and the hair texture to be dressed.

12.12 THE CLIENT AND BACKDRESSING

Unless the client is shown how to deal with her backdressed hair, difficulty may be met when trying to cope with it. A few words on correct combing and brushing techniques will help considerably, enabling the client to remove backdressing without tearing or breaking the hair.

12.13 DRESSING LONG HAIR

Dressing long hair in downward positions is not difficult if the hair is cut into a good shape: the hair will hang well if it is in good condition. Long, flowing styles may be best finished with a hand dryer.

When dressing long hair into upswept positions it is important to centralise the weight. This enables the hair to stay in position without falling. Once placed, it should be secured with pins, grips, rubber bands, combs, ribbons or plaited hair: care must be taken when these are secured not to damage the hair. If the hair is to be plaited small sections should be taken and angled so that the desired portions are achieved. When the weight and bulk of the hair is positioned and secured the lengths may then be dressed; care should be taken not to disturb the firmness of the base.

12.14 DRESSING A PLEAT

After brushing the hair the top crown hair should be secured and placed out of the way – the side hair may be dressed separately or dressed in with the back. The back hair is positioned, smoothed, and then secured into place. The pleat is then folded and placed, either centrally or diagonally. The hair may first be backdressed for added fullness.

If the pleat is to be placed to the left or right of the centre back the hair should be brushed initially in that direction. The hand is then placed on the head, at the angle the pleat is to lie and the hair firmly gripped into position. The hair is then brushed and placed on to the palm of one hand, which grasps and supports the bulk of the hair. The other hand, after releasing the brush, takes hold of the hair ends and directs them towards the head. At the same time the hand should be moving up to the crown, which helps to spread the hair. The hand resting on the head can then be released, which assists in finally positioning the pleat. Securing of the pleat with pins and grips should be done at the edges and in a way that does not become obvious.

Make sure the head is in an upright position before placing the pleat – any forward head movement will tend to tighten, rather than loosen, the pleat, but if the pleat is placed when the head is too far forward it will loosen when the head becomes erect. After securing the pleat the sides and top may then be dressed. This may be done in a variety of ways: the front or crown hair may be dressed to cover the top part of the pleat, the sides may be waved back, curled, draped or placed into ringlets. The pleat is a frequently used dressing for long hair and is often called a French roll (Figure 12.4(a)–(d)) on pp. 176-7.

12.15 PLAITING

Plaiting is a useful way of dealing with long hair. A variety of sizes and shapes of plaits may be used and attractively positioned; basket weave effects have again achieved popularity. The wigmaker of the past was usually the expert at plaiting and weaving tresses. Plaiting is achieved by intertwining a variety of hair sections together, one over the other. The three-stem plait is commonly used. Small or large, with two or more stems, may be attractively placed.

12.16 ORNAMENTS AND DRESSING

Various ornaments have been used over the years to complete dressings: combs, ribbons, jewels, grips, slides and a varied range of shapes and materials have been used to enhance the dressed head of hair. Added hair pieces are an attractive means of ornamentation, so too are flowers, feathers, glitterdust, colour sprays, beads and sequins amongst others.

Hair pieces of many kinds are useful in hair dressing. Apart from their uses in covering injuries, scars, bald patches or other defects, hair pieces can be decorative and interesting. The means of securing hair pieces vary, most being attached by combs, grips or pins. Styled wigs can be used to make a complete change of dressing. For the range and variety of hair pieces available reference should be made to textbooks of hair pieces or postiche.

12.17 DRESSING AIDS

The tools, materials, and chemicals used each have their effect on the hair. Lacquer may be added to give 'body' to the hair; it 'fixes' the shape and helps to retain the dressed shape longer by resisting the effects of moisture. Most lacquers are easily removed by washing but some are more difficult to remove and build up on the hair. These require special lacquer solvents to be applied, usually before washing the hair.

Lacquer should be sprayed on to the hair from a distance of about 300mm. This ensures an even distribution of the lacquer. If sprays are tilted a stream of lacquer may be ejected, and if sprayed too close, too much will be deposited on the hair. This causes the hair to become wet, lacquer beads to form, the set to loosen, and the dressing to be spoilt. Use just enough lacquer to do the job required without overloading.

Precautions to be taken when using lacquer:

(1) Avoid using, or storing, lacquer near naked flames, since it is inflammable and a fire may easily be started.
(2) Shield eyes to prevent lacquer being sprayed into them, avoiding discomfort and irritation.
(3) Cover and protect clients' clothes.
(4) Keep lacquer spray clean and do not allow the opening to become blocked.
(5) Never remove a blockage from an aerosol spray with a pin or the end of a tailcomb. Lacquer is packed under pressure and if anything is poked into the spray opening the container could explode and cause damage, particularly to the eyes and face. A little spirit may be used to soften and remove a dried lacquer blockage.

Control creams, oils and gels may be used to add gloss, bind hair, reduce static electricity and enable the hair to be combed smoothly. These are made from a wide variety of materials, some in aerosol sprays, but they must be used sparingly; the application of too much control material can spoil the finished dressing and make the hair lank and greasy.

Static electricity is produced by the friction movements of combing and brushing. This causes the hair to 'fly away'. Gentle stroking with the hand, the back of the comb, or the help of another type of comb, helps to restrict this.

Natural shine on the hair is due to the smoothness of the hair surface and the natural oil of the glands of the scalp. This oil is called sebum. It is formed in the glands – the sebaceous glands – surrounding the hair follicle. If the hair surface is smooth, light will reflect from the oily surface, to give the gloss or shine. The rougher the surface, the duller the hair will appear.

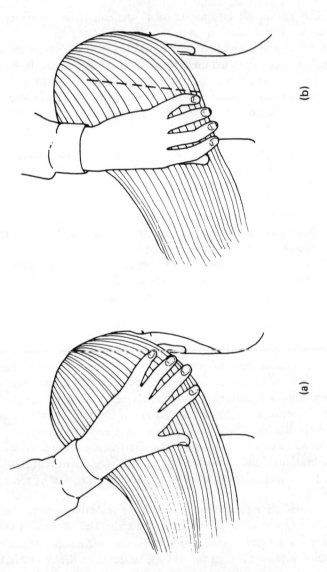

Fig 12.4 (a) – (b) *dressing a pleat, showing correct hair/hand/head positions*

(a)

(b)

177

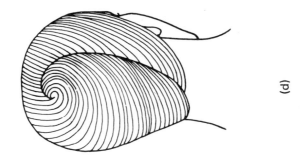

(d)

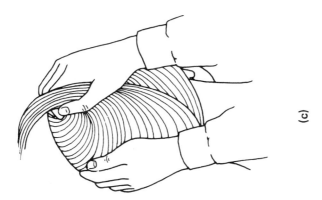

(c)

Fig 12.4(c)–(d)

12.18 THE FINAL LOOK

The beauty of a well-dressed head of hair is dependent on the cutting, the condition and the final finish, including the position of the distributed hair, or the style shape produced. The dressing should combine the lines and movements within the shape so that they flow throughout. The forms produced should lighten the face and head, and remove flat, odd shapes, which may be dull and uninteresting.

Each dressing technique is finally dependent on the artistic placing of the hair. This should fit the pattern imagined or created by the dresser. The final dressed shape should reflect artistic appreciation, usually acquired through hard work and practice.

Dressing and hairstyling are very closely interlinked and the artistic application of both is essential for the production of good work. So too are a study of the practical techniques involved, and the client's face and head, for style and fashionable dressing to be acceptable.

EXERCISES

1 What is meant by 'dressing the hair'?
2 Describe the tools used for dressing.
3 What are the techniques involved with dressing?
4 What is the difference between dressing and styling?
5 What is meant by the term 'overdressing'?
6 What is ornamentation?
7 What causes the hair to become 'flyaway', and how can it be dealt with?
8 Describe a method of dressing.
9 Describe the difference of three types of dressing.
10 What precautions should be taken when using lacquer?

HAIR STYLING

13.1 HAIR STYLING

Designing or creating hair shapes or arrangements is called hair styling.
This involves good cutting, placing and dressing. A hair style is an expression of form and shape. It is achieved by arranging the hair into suitable,
balanced lines which complement the underlying face and head structures.
Hair that does not follow this pattern cannot be considered to be well
styled.

The aim of the hair style is to improve the appearance of the wearer,
helping to make the client feel good and boosting confidence. The hair
style should fit the occasion for which it is intended to be worn. There are
styles for work, play, special dates, meetings and events. It should be considered a part of the complete ensemble: clothes, make-up and accessories.

13.2 HAIR STYLE DESIGN

Hair style design is dependent on: the shape of face and head; the features
of the face, head, and body; dress, and the occasion for the style; quality
and quantity of the hair; the age of client and the hair position, proportion
and form in relation to other styling requirements.

The shape of the face and head is the base on which the hair shape will
rest. The proportions, balance and distribution of hair should bear some
relation to the underlying structure and features. Eyes, nose, chin, etc.
should be used as a guide to the finished hair shape.

When looking at the head from the front the outline of the face forms
an inner shape. This outline describes a particular individual shape and
these inner shapes vary: some are round, some oval, oblong and heart-shaped. Others are square, triangular, and diamond-shaped. Many are
mixtures of these shapes. The oval shape is considered the ideal since most
hair style shapes fit it. The apparent length of square or oblong faces may

be accentuated by sleek, flat styles or diminished by fullness at the sides. The large, round face looks rounder when even, framing shapes are dressed, but longer when the hair is dressed higher in the front. Hard-looking face shapes, with prominent jawbones, appear harder when the hair is dressed back, but softer when forward hair movements are used (Figure 13.1 and 13.2).

Fig 13.1   *oval face shape*

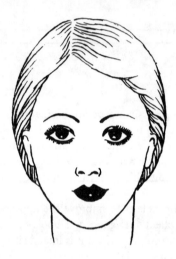

Fig 13.2   *round face shape*

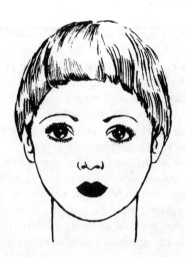

The shape of the head, and the proportion of the head above the face, is another hairstyling consideration. This applies particularly when dressing the top and front hair. The roundness or flatness of the back of the head and the profile, which features the chin, mouth, nose, eyes and forehead, all affect the look of the style (Figure 13.3).

Fig 13.3 *variation of head and face shape*

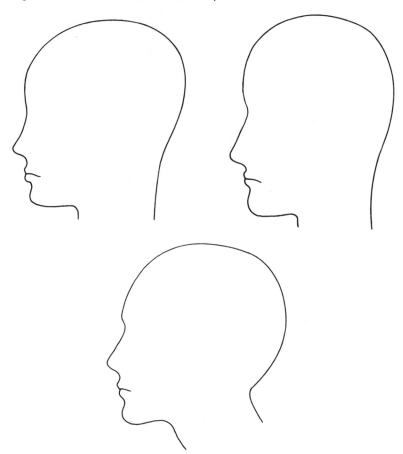

The neck - its length, fullness and width - directly affects the fall of the back and nape hair. Different head positions affect the style and must be considered (Figure 13.4).

The features of the face, head and body help to determine the hair style. A prominent, large or badly-placed nose may be 'diminished' by dressing the front hair at an angle, or avoiding a centre parting. Square

Fig 13.4 *neck shapes – swan and short*

jawlines may be softened by full side dressings, and protruding ears are best covered. Wrinkled eyes are made more obvious when straight, hardline dressings are used, yet they may be diminished by softly angling the hair away. Low, high, wide or narrow foreheads may be disguised by angling the hair and varying the fringe positions. A common fault when trying to hide a defect is to make it more obvious by using too much hair to hide it (Figure 13.5(a) and (b)).

Fig 13.5 *profile showing accentuated nose. Nose accentuated by style line*

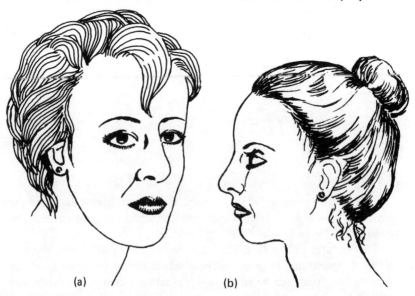

(a)   (b)

Hollow cheeks may be 'improved' by dressing fuller side hair, but if the cheeks are prominent then fullness will need to be dressed higher to achieve balance. Chin shapes are softened by longer hair, but hardened by directing the hair towards them. The shape of facial features, and the lines and shadows cast by them, should be used to counterbalance the hair bulk and to enhance and soften overall effects.

A large, fussy hair style on a big-built person can look unsightly. Yet a small, head-hugging style may be completely out of proportion. Care is necessary to balance the body shape and the hair proportions. High styles accentuated a person's height and a flat style on a short person will make the lack of height more noticeable and the 'right look' is attained only after careful consideration. It is also important to note the size, shape and characteristics of the person. Take note of the way the head is normally held and whether the body is held erect, etc. These points are best observed when first receiving the client, and certainly before any work is started.

Dress and occasion

The dress and occasion for which the style is to be worn helps to determine the style dressed. The clothes worn and the work done by receptionists, office workers or the busy housewife should influence the hair style designed. There are many occasions, e.g. work, play, dates, interviews, visits, which require different styles to be dressed. Styles for demonstrations, displays or photography require special styling. A style suitable for a theatre visit will differ from one worn at work. A beautiful evening gown requires an elegant hair style, and normal working clothes require smart, suitable and practical styles. Hairdressers should wear hair styles which set an example for their suitability, practicability and good choice.

Many clients require styles that are suitable and easy to manage, but for the special event practicability is less essential since the style needs to suit the event only. Generally, the smart, unexaggerated, suitable and practical styles are best used for everyday occasions and the more elaborate ones left for the special events.

Usually, lower necklines require longer hair styles, and higher necklines allow higher dressings. There are exceptions, such as dancing competitors, who require balanced dressings to complete their ensemble, or ice skaters, who will not want loose, flowing styles that will impede movement or vision.

The quality and quantity of hair is reflected in all hair styles: bad texture and condition never looks attractive. Shining, healthy hair is essential for good hairstyling. Hair condition is affected by the care given to the hair, and the use of many processes and materials.

Thin, scanty hair is difficult to dress and requires a great deal of attention. Good cutting, placing and careful handling is necessary with this type of hair. Styles which make it appear thicker and fuller are usually successful. Very fine, thin hair is soon affected by damp air and loses its shape. Setting aids and practical dressings are needed for this hair type. Dry, thick hair requires sleeker, smooth styles to contain it. This type of hair soon fluffs and loses shape. Control dressings and less backdressing usually help.

Each *age group* requires different special effects or styles. The young can take most styles: good, and often odd, effects are used by this group. Straight, curled, long, short, hard and soft effects may be used to advantage. Young styles are often opposing current trends and trying to set their own effect. Teenage fashion does not generally include the styles of older women.

The young married woman requires suitable, practical and stylish shapes. She is more inclined to fashion trends and is probably at an age when they may best be used. More extreme, as well as more glamorous hair styles, are requested by this group. Career women go for fashionable, attractive shapes which they wear as part of their everyday dress.

Older women require greater consideration for suitable styling. Here facial features, lines and wrinkles need to be 'styled out', and made less obvious. Correctly planned styles, usually with more movement, are much in demand. The elegance of the older well-dressed and styled woman is much admired and probably reflects good hair styling more than any other age.

Hair position, proportion and form cannot be considered in the absence of other aspects of styling, or the techniques of dressing. The outline that the hair forms in relation to the shape of the face contributes to the 'look' of the combined shapes. Dressing varies the hair shape and can be changed repeatedly to fit. It is important that balance of the hair position and face shape is attained. This needs to be closely viewed, from all sides, particularly in profile.

13.3 STYLING REQUIREMENTS

These involve an understanding of suitability, balance, line, movement, softness and hardness of shapes and of appearance. Originality is a much used term which, amongst others, needs some defining.

Suitability is the effect of the hair shape on the face, and features of the head and body. A hair style is usually suitable when it looks right. A line of the face may be accentuated when the hair lines are continuous with it, and softened when they are angled away. The more the unwanted features are highlighted the less suitable the style will be.

A young, fashionable style dressed on the older woman can be most unattractive. This is because the lines of face, eyes and forehead are accentuated by the harder lines of the 'younger' style. Most fashion styles are designed for the young woman and require to be adapted to meet the needs of the older woman. The most suitable style is the one individually designed.

Balance is the effect produced by the amount, fullness and distribution of hair throughout the style. Symmetrical balance is achieved when the hair is similarly placed on both sides of the head. Asymmetrical balance can be achieved by dressing long hair to one side of the head and countering the weight with one earing on the other. Here the lines and proportions created by the dressing produce the balanced 'look'. The hair style should be balanced from all sides of the head (Figure 13.6).

The *line* of a style is the direction, or directions, in which the hair is positioned. Line should follow throughout the shape. If the line suddenly ends, the style varies, becomes unbalanced, and the wrong effect is produced. The line of the style is affected by the way in which it fits, or otherwise, with the lines of the facial features and contours. The line of the style will carry the eye of the viewer along the directions the hair is placed. Many style lines produce illusionary effects by accentuating or diminishing different features. The dressings of well known hair stylists are instances of the use of good style line (Figure 13.7).

The lines produced by partings in the hair have their effect. A long, straight central parting appears to make the nose more prominent, but a short, angled parting will 'diminish' a prominent nose. Round, fat faces

Fig 13.6 *balance*

appear bigger with central partings, smaller with a side parting (Figure 13.8(a) and (b)).

Movement is the variation of direction of the style line. The more varied the line, the more movement there will be. Curl or wave displays movement. The line of a style should move from one point of the head to another in a fluid fashion to the ends of the hair. Styles with movement are usually complementary to the older woman. Contrasting, straight line styles are more effective on the young, for their sharp line, hardness and impact.

Soft and hard effects are dependent on suitably balanced lines and movements. Hair dressed without divisions, sudden variations of line, or abrupt finish to movement, will look soft and natural. Careful colouring will further enhance soft effects but careless colouring can produce hard, unwanted effects. Rhythmical movement and balancing is softening. Lack of movement and irregular, unbalanced shape produces hard style effects (Figure 13.9).

Originality in salon styling is restricted to individual styling. Creating a new style line requires a great deal of thought and work but adapting styles and fashion lines creates some interesting, sometimes original, variations. Enabling styles to fit individuals, without aiming at fashion replicas, can be more satisfying and satisfactory. Displays, demonstrations and hairdressing competitions offer opportunities for original styling.

Fig 13.7   *style line or line of style*

Fig 13.8(a) and (b)   *balance and partings*

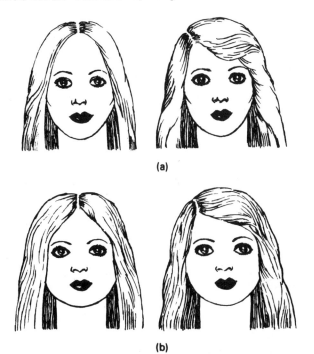

(a)

(b)

Fig **13.9** *hard line – Egyptian*

13.4 **PERSONAL CHOICE**

The stylist's personal choice plays a large part in styling. New styles are often disliked *because* they are new and not understood and there is often reluctance to adopt new lines. Personal choice may be against new lines, but when adopted, they may prove to be correct and pleasing. Personal style preference is acceptable in a stylist provided the style range is not restricted by it. A varied clientele requires a range of styles. Different lines, shapes, effects and variations are requested by different clients and stylists may become known for their particular form of styling. Others become equally well known for their range and adaptability. A few individual hair stylists work to their own original lines and invariably deserve the acclaim they receive. The successful stylist's personal choice of styling is usually based on hard practice, technical ability and artistic appreciation.

13.5 **THE PERSONALITY OF THE CLIENT**

This may be reflected in the client's hair style and it should be used to create individual differences of shape. Each client has her own mannerisms, appeal and attractiveness. Some are smiling and active and may wear more adventuresome styles; the mature, smart client requires more sophisticated hair styles; and older clients require elegant, simple, graceful shapes to enhance their personalities.

13.6 SALON STYLING

Salon styling requires a range of styles which depend on the clientele in existence, or to be attracted. Some salons cater for all kinds of clients, others for a certain age range or type. The more varied the techniques and abilities of the stylist, the more varied and larger the clientele becomes. The good stylist is nearly always appreciated and in demand.

13.7 TYPES OF HAIR STYLE

These vary according to the occasion for which they are to be worn. The following are some of those in general use.

A *day style* is usually a simple, suitable and practical shape for wearing during the day. Day styles should be attractive, uncluttered and easy to manage, without extreme ornamentation, colour or elaboration. Some of the 'young' styles are an exception.

The *cocktail style* is the name given to a more exaggerated day style. It should be suitable for wear at a special meeting or date during the daytime or evening. Ornaments and colour variations may be used.

Evening styles are generally more elaborate shapes. Not necessarily practical, but suitable for wear at dances, parties or special occasions. The style line is usually augmented with colour or ornamentation; the occasion and boldness of the wearer determining the elaboration of style required.

High fashion or haute coiffure, refers to the latest trends in hair styling. These may at first appear extreme, and are often disliked, but are usually accepted as the fashion becomes understood, worn and seen. High fashion styling requires originality, good technique and experience. High fashion styles are designed for certain types of model and are not suitable for wear by the majority without adaptation.

Fashion styles are usually adapted high fashion styles and are favoured by the smart or trendy type of person. The constant demand for fashion change is stimulated by an endless variety of events, mood, habit and the wish to be different.

Children's styling is required to be natural, never artificial, and in suitable shapes. The degree of finish usually desired by women is rarely wanted for children: the simpler the shape the better.

Men's styling is based on similar principles to those used for women's styling. Men's shapes should be natural, fitting, suitable, balanced, practical and well finished. They are not usually as elaborate as women's at the present time, but fashions can change in a short space of time.

13.8 COMPETITION STYLING

This type of styling is intended for display on the competition floor and differs from salon styling. Much, however, is derived from competition work which is most helpful in the salon.

There are local, regional, national and international competitions with varying requirements: international events are usually at a high level. Each competition requires a specific type of styling, e.g. day, cocktail or evening, and free-style competitions allow any style to be dressed. There are competitions for cutting, colour, perming and other techniques.

Those wishing to enter competitions need to know what is required before entering. The rules of the competition are available from the organisers. These rules must be followed or disqualification could occur. Competitions vary to allow for the degree of experience: the junior competitions cater for the less experienced while the senior ones allow for past winners, etc. to compete. The best way to start is to attend the local competitions and by watching, listening and generally taking part a lot can be learned.

Choice of a suitable model for entry to competitions is important, and however good the model, styling ability must be practised. This also applies to the style to be entered. The time it takes to complete the dressing and the finish of the style should be well rehearsed. The style chosen must conform to the competition rules, and exceptions must be determined by the organisers.

EXERCISES

1 What is a hair style?
2 Describe how a suitable hair style may be chosen.
3 What is meant by a 'suitable' hair style?
4 What is meant by the 'line' of the style?
5 How do the shape, and features, of the face and head affect hair styling?
6 How does the age of a client affect the choice of a style?
7 What is meant by 'balance' in a hair style?
8 How are personality, clothes and special events features in choosing a hair style?
9 What is meant by 'movement' in a hair style?
10 What are the differences between 'salon' and 'high fashion' styling?

HAIR COLOURING

14.1 HAIR COLOURING

Hair colouring is the process of adding to or altering the natural hair colour. It is used to disguise or cover grey and white hair, and to enhance or completely change the natural shade. Hair colourings have been used for centuries, in one form or another, to produce different effects for various reasons and in recent times it has become popular for both men and women to use hair colouring cosmetics for fashion and style effects.

The field of modern hair colouring is wide, and may be separated into two main divisions: (1) the addition of hair colourings, e.g. tinting and (2) the removal of natural and synthetic hair colouring, e.g. bleaching and de-colouring.

Artificial and synthetic colourings added to hair are grouped according to the length of time they remain on the hair. These are: *temporary colourings, semi-permanent colourings* and *permanent tints or colours.* A summary of the different colourings is given in the figure on page 210.

14.2 TEMPORARY COLOURINGS

These are obtained in several forms: rinses in concentrated solutions, setting lotions, hair colour lacquer, sprays, crayons, paint and glitterdust. These remain on the hair until washed or shampooed. They do not usually penetrate the hair or directly affect the natural colour. This type of colouring coats the surface of the hair only, but some may be absorbed by very porous and poor condition hair (Figure 14.1).

Temporary rinses consist of dilutions of the colour concentrate, i.e. a few drops are added to a measured quantity of water. The mixtures vary according to the instructions and the colour depth required. The liquid rinse produced is applied with a brush or sponge; or by being repeatedly poured through. Hot water should be used to dilute, to ensure that it will

Fig 14.1 *temporary colouring*

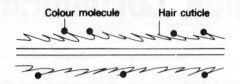

Colour molecule   Hair cuticle

cling to the hair. For sponge or brush applications the hair should be sub-divided into 6–8mm sections, and the rinse evenly and repeatedly distributed.

Premixed temporary rinses are available which are applied to the hair after shampooing and allowed to dry on the hair. These are based on the traditional water rinses and used in the same way.

Advantages of temporary rinses are:

(a) the temporary colour effect
(b) ease of removal
(c) the conditioning properties
(d) the subtle toning effects on grey, white and normal hair
(e) the fashion effects on bleached hair.

Hair colour setting lotions are one of the most popular forms of temporary colouring. The shades are incorporated in suitable setting agents with which the hair may be set. No mixing is required, or dilution, and they may be applied with a sponge, brush or poured directly from the bottle. The lotion is distributed through the hair by frictioning with the fingertips. It is important to towel dry the hair before the application of these lotions or the excess water will dilute the colour.

The advantages of coloured setting lotions are:

(a) the range of colours
(b) the variety of setting agents for different hair types
(c) they allow colour to be more easily introduced to the client
(d) they are easily removed by washing.

Coloured hair lacquers are temporary colourings which can be sprayed on dry, dressed hair. These products have a restricted colour range but there are several suitable colourings available.

Hair colour sprays are made in liquid and powder form, in various colours, for use on dry, dressed hair. They coat the hair cuticle from which they are easily removed by brushing or washing. Some of these colourings are metallic, e.g. gold, silver or bronze, and other metallic colours are popularly used. Care must be taken when using them on blonde, white and bleached hair or discoloration may result.

Hair colour crayons and paints are mainly used for their theatrical effects. Periodically they become popular and more generally used: they are particularly useful for highlighting a dressing.

Glitterdust is made of glittering or shining coloured metal dust which, when sprinkled on the hair, produces a twinkling, sparkling effect. Gold and silver are most commonly used, and though a temporary colour effect is attained, glitterdust is, strictly, an ornamentation.

14.3 SEMI-PERMANENT COLOURINGS

These colourings are made in liquid and cream forms, and need no mixing. The addition of water or hydrogen peroxide is not required. They are deposited in the hair cuticle, where they remain longer than temporary colours, but the colour gradually lifts each time the hair is washed: some last through six to eight shampoos. Although not intended to cover a large percentage of white hair, these colourings do so to a greater extent than temporary colourings (Figure 14.2).

Fig 14.2 *semi-permanent colouring*

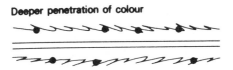

Deeper penetration of colour

The colour range is varied, but careful choice is necessary as, for instance, a black rinse on white hair will not produce pleasing results, and subtle effects will not be achieved. Timing and development are affected by the salon temperature and the texture and porosity of the hair. Heat and poor hair condition may speed absorption.

Preparation for semi-permanent colour applications is as follows. The hair should be shampooed with a suitable shampoo, preferably one specially made for pre-colouring. Remove the excess water by thoroughly towel drying. This helps to prevent dilution of the colour. The scalp should always be checked for cuts, sores or other abnormalities which may be aggravated by the colouring, and suitable protective coverings should be used for both client and operator.

Application may be made with a sponge, brush or application bottle, or poured direct from the container on to the hair. The colouring should be evenly applied and the hair left loose on the head to allow for air circulation and even development of the colour. Steamers or accelerators may be used to speed processing. Heat should not be used without covering the hair, preferably with a plastic cap, or the colouring will dry out and this will prevent the colour reaching the depth and evenness required.

Stains may be caused on dry skin and these can be removed with toilet spirit or specially made removers. Barrier creams or Vaseline can be applied to the hairline before application to prevent bright, noticeable staining.

Advantages of semi-permanent colourings are:

(1) They are more effective and longer lasting than most temporary colourings.
(2) A larger colour range and choice is available.
(3) Root regrowth is not noticeable since the colour will have lifted by the time the contrasting hair has grown.
(4) Natural hair colour is not directly affected.
(5) Skin tests are not usually required with this type of colouring, but there are some semi-permanents that do require skin testing. Always check instructions before use.
(6) Foaming agents contained help prevent the liquid from running off the hair.
(7) Various types are made and it is important that instructions for their use are followed for good results.

Some permanent colourings may be diluted or mixed to produce semi-permanent effects. These products contain substances which are known skin irritants and should not be used without testing skin reaction first. Mixtures of this type of rinse should only be made on the manufacturer's recommendation.

14.4 PERMANENT COLOURINGS

There is a wide variety of these colourings available. The modern oxidation colourings are made in cream form, semi-viscous, and liquid forms. Most colourings used for tinting need to be mixed with hydrogen peroxide – without this they would be completely ineffective. These products are used to cover white, grey and most natural hair colour to produce other natural, fantasy or exotic colours and fashion shades.

Tinting consists of making the synthetic colouring penetrate the hair cuticle, and be absorbed into the cortex. This is where the colour is oxidised and remains permanently fixed and the natural hair colour is affected by the lightening action of the oxidation process. Although the colour effects are permanent, the choice of product, effects of weather and growth of hair all affect its lasting qualities (Figure 14.3).

Fig 14.3 *permanent colouring*

14.5 COLOUR CHOICE

Choice of colour is determined by the following:

(a) the texture of the hair
(b) the porosity of the hair
(c) the condition of the hair
(d) the amount of natural colouring present, referred to as the natural base shade
(e) the client's requirements
(f) the client's natural skin colour
(g) the type of colouring used
(h) the shade of colour desired.

Hair texture, or the various thicknesses of hair, affects the degree of tint absorption. Generally, fine hair takes a tint quicker and more readily than does thick, coarse hair.

Porosity indicates the amount the hair will take up liquids and materials. The condition of the hair affects its porosity. Poor condition hair, for example, with the cuticle torn and lifted, quickly absorbs large amounts of a tint, which may cause unevenness of colour. Other states or conditions of hair may resist tint absorption, e.g., closely packed cuticle cells resist the colour and loosely packed ones allow penetration (Figure 14.4).

Fig 14.4 *cuticle – closed and open*

Closed cuticle

Open cuticle

Natural hair colour is contained mainly in the cortex. It is composed of colour pigments in the form of granules called melanin. Four basic colours are contained in varying amounts in each shade, i.e., black, brown, red and yellow. Pheomelanin is the name given to the red and yellow pigments, which are smaller than the black and brown melanin cells.

Varying quantities of colour pigment produce different hair shades. Dark brown hair contains more melanin and less pheomelanin. Light ash blonde contains less black and brown pigment with a greater amount of yellow than red colour pigment. Ash or drab shades are determined by the quantity of red pigment present and contain less than the gold or warm shades (Figure 14.5).

Grey or white hair contains little or no melanin. The less melanin, the whiter the hair. The amount of white or grey hairs in a head is usually expressed as a percentage. If every other hair is white or grey it is said there is 50% white hair present. Approximate percentages may be arrived at and used to determine the choice of colour, e.g., a red tint applied to 70% grey hair could produce a gaudy, unnatural colour.

Albino hair is completely white owing to the absence of melanin. This is usually due to the body being unable to make and distribute the melanin. The colour may also be absent from the skin and eyes, when the condition is known as albinism. Partial albinism is similar, but with some colour pigment present in the hair, eyes and skin.

The *client's choice of colour* should not be ignored. It may be necessary to use clashing colours for a particular reason or event, for example a theatrical stage part, but for normal colouring the natural blending shades are best used.

Skin colour helps to determine the choice of a suitable synthetic hair colour. A deep red tint on the hair will clash with a red or ruddy skin complexion. As with hair, the colour of skin is also determined by the amount of melanin present; the darker the skin the more melanin is contained. Sunlight will vary the amount of melanin, particularly in lighter skin colours, e.g. white skin becomes 'tanned' in sunny weather. This is Nature's way of giving extra protection to the underlying skin tissues against the ultra violet rays in sunlight (Figure 14.6, p. 198).

The *type of colouring used* may vary considerably. Modern colourings are comparatively simple to apply and good results are achieved if correctly chosen, mixed and timed. The choice of a light temporary colouring on dark hair would be wrong because the colour would be absorbed. This is an example of incorrect colour choice and type.

The *shade of colour desired* often determines the type and choice of colour. A white-haired client may require a slightly toned effect, without heaviness. Here the temporary and semi-permanent colourings may be suitable. Newer additions to the permanent colour ranges may be used to

Fig 14.5 *melanin and pheomelanin*

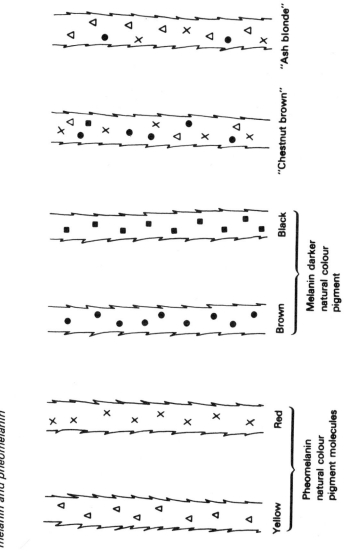

Fig 14.6 *skin tan – ultra-violet rays*

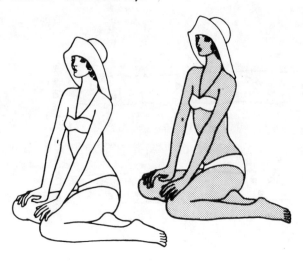

produce, for example, silver, pewter, blue and violet tone effects. Emphasis should be placed on the use of lighter, rather than heavy and dark, colourings for white hair on the older type of skin, lacking in colour, in order to avoid clashing.

14.6 SKIN REACTION

Most permanent colourings contain substances that will irritate some types of skin. The skin should be tested 24–28 hours before the application of this type of colourant. This is to determine the skin reaction to the colourant. A skin test should be made periodically to assess tolerance to the colourant, as it is possible for clients regularly having colour treatments to react to the material used, and their skin should be tested before each tint is applied.

A client is more likely, though this is not always the case, to react to tinting products if they are allergic to other substances, such as washing up detergents, lipsticks or some types of food. Colourings containing potentially irritating substances should clearly state this on the label and in the instructions for its use because of the possibility of skin reaction.

A *skin test*, alternatively called a predisposition test, patch test or Sabouraud-Rousseau test, is carried out as follows:

(1) Mix a small amount of the tint to be used with the correct strength of hydrogen peroxide.

(2) Clean an area of skin approximately 10mm square behind the ear, or

in the fold of the arm. A little spirit on cotton wool will remove the grease from the skin.

(3) Apply a little of the tint to the area and allow to dry.

(4) The patch of tint can then be covered with collodion, which forms a protective film when dry.

(5) The client should be asked to report any discomfort or irritation in the following 24 to 48 hours.

(6) The client must be seen during this period so that any signs of reaction are not missed.

(7) If there is any skin reaction, i.e. inflammation, swelling, irritation or discomfort, in the area of the skin test, then no colouring treatment should be carried out.

(8) If this reaction to the skin test is ignored, a more serious reaction could result if tinting treatment is given. Under these circumstances no colourings containing these irritants should be applied.

(9) If there is no skin reaction to the patch test, i.e., no itching, soreness or inflammation, the colouring treatment can be carried out.

14.7 PREPARATION OF THE HAIR

Preparation is made more efficient if all materials and equipment are placed ready for use. Towels, protective coverings for client and operator, glass measures, dishes, applicators, combs, cotton wool and rubber gloves should all be at hand. The colourants are selected and checked after the colour choice has been made; always check that the correct tube is in the correct box, etc.

Sectioning the hair from centre forehead to nape, and from ear to ear across the crown, should be done before mixing the tint. Subsections approximately 6mm wide are taken when the tint is applied, usually starting at the nape. Hair in the lower parts of the head, beneath the top layers of hair, is usually darker and more resistant to tinting than the upper layers. This is due to the effects of combing, brushing and sunlight which lighten or lift the cuticle and make the hair porous.

Mixing the colour should not be done by guesswork; it should be prepared carefully as directed and the correct quantities accurately measured. The wrong proportions may produce unwanted colour effects. Prepare the tint immediately before use – do not allow it to stand for any length of time or the material loses its effectiveness.

Application of the tint should be evenly distributed and each subsection well covered. Using too little material produces varying colour effects, and too much tint applied results in waste, but good coverage of the hair is essential for good results.

Cream tints, usually applied with a brush, should not be applied with a scraping action. The tint should be laid on the section and should not then be scraped off again with the brush. The tint container should be placed near to the client. This will help to prevent any of the tint dripping on to the client or the floor. Semi-viscous and liquid tints may be applied with a sponge, applicator brush, bottle or dispenser. The application of the tint is varied by its thickness or thinness. The more liquid the tint, the larger the sections which may be taken, because it penetrates the hair section quicker. Smaller sections need to be taken if the tint mixture is thicker. For controlled effects the applicator brush is commonly used.

Processing, or development timing, usually begins when the application is complete and this must be accurately timed. If too little time is given to development the tint or result will be underprocessed, i.e., not complete, and the wrong colours will be produced. Too much time given to development may, with some colouring products, result in overprocessing, i.e., too dark shades being produced. Steamers and accelerators may be used to speed the processing, which when complete should be tested for the colour result. This is done by testing a strand of hair.

A *hair strand test* consists of removing the tint from a strand of hair by lightly rubbing with a paper tissue or the back of the comb. This is then compared with any untinted part of the head of hair for evenness and similarity. If the result is even throughout the length of hair strand the tint can be removed. If there is unevenness, further development is indicated or more tint needs to be applied. It is important to allow most colouring products the recommended processing time for good colour to be attained.

Removing the tint depends on the type of tint used. Some require the addition of a little water, light massage and rinsing. Others may require shampooing. Stains on the skin may be removed by the addition of some of the tint direct to the stain. This softens the stain, which is then easily removed with water. Do not allow the tint to remain too long on the skin or deepening of the stain will result. The hair should not be ruffled at this stage or tangling will result.

Colour result should be checked when the hair is dry. The colour of the hair in a set state appears darker. By rubbing the hair with a towel to remove the water, the colour result can be seen.

14.8 TINTING IN PRACTICE

Procedure will vary for a first time tint and a regrowth tint. Commencement of application will also vary according to the natural base shade, the resultant colour required and the hair porosity.

Virgin hair is hair that has not been chemically treated or tinted. A first-time application on virgin hair requires a specific application method. *Regrowth tinting*, often called a retouch, consists of applying the tint to the hair that has regrown since the last tint.

Tinting virgin hair requires the tint application to be made first to the mid-lengths, i.e., the main part of the hair. Then it is applied to the points, ie., the last 25mm of the hair tips. Finally application is made to the roots i.e., the remaining hair about 12.25mm from the head. This allows for the varying degrees of porosity throughout the hair length. The hair points are naturally lighter, particularly on long hair, due to wear and weather. The root ends are closest to the head and heat from the head activates the tint more quickly. The mid-lengths are usually more resistant and will absorb the tint more slowly (Figure 14.7).

Fig 14.7 *application of tint to virgin hair*

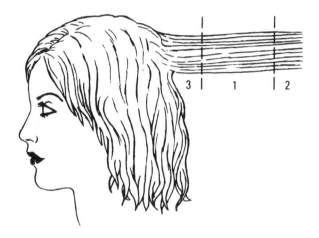

With the use of steamers and accelerators it is possible to level out development by causing the hair to absorb the colouring at an even rate. This reduces the development time by half.

Regrowth tinting is the application of tint to the hair grown since the last processing. By retouching, i.e., tinting regrowth only, the colour is maintained. The tint is applied to the regrowth, allowed to process and then removed from the hair. The mid-lengths and points should not be processed each time the regrowth is retouched. This can only result in over-processed and poor condition hair.

Combing through after a regrowth tint is permissible with some colouring products. To achieve this the tint is diluted with water, or water is added to the hair, and combed through the hair. This maintains an even colour and corrects any colour lifting from the hair since the last tint. Repeatedly combing *undiluted* tint through the hair after each regrowth tint should not be done, as it affects the hair and resultant colour.

Tinting darker or lighter is possible with modern oxidation tints, by adding to, or lightening, the natural hair shade. The difference between the two is the natural base shade to be treated, the synthetic colour chosen and the hydrogen peroxide strength used.

A client with light brown hair may require a darker shade. The colour choice is made by considering the texture, porosity, condition, percentage of grey, etc., and a brown or dark brown colour may be used. Since the natural colour shade is to be darkened it will not be necessary to use a high strength oxidant.

If the client requires a lighter shade, a stronger oxidant will be necessary to lighten the natural darker pigments and oxidise the lighter synthetic colour in the hair. If the degree of lightening is to be too many shades below the natural colour, for example, lightening from black to light blonde, then pre-bleaching should be carried out first.

Resistant hair is hair that does not readily absorb tint. It is usually better to apply the tint to any known resistant parts first so that they receive a longer processing time. White hair may be resistant, but usually it is more porous and tint needs to be applied to it last of all. This applies particularly if warm or red shades are being used. It may be necessary to pre-soften resistant hair by applying diluted hydrogen peroxide and ammonium hydroxide. This makes it more porous by causing the cuticle to lift.

The resistance or porosity of the hair may be determined by developing a 'feel' for the hair. Touching the hair should tell an experienced hairdresser its condition, from which its porosity may be assessed. Rough hair is more likely to be porous.

Other factors help to determine resistance or porosity. These are listed as follows:

(a) hair which usually takes a perm quickly
(b) recently permed hair
(c) hair which curls easily and tightly
(d) previously coloured hair
(e) dry hair
(f) bleached hair.

Hair more likely to be resistant is as follows:

(a) hair which soon drops out of set
(b) hair that takes perms slowly
(c) greasy hair
(d) smooth surface hair, with a tightly packed cuticle.

Occasionally, fine hair can be highly resistant, but it usually takes colour quickly.

14.9 COMPETITION AND FANTASY COLOURING

This technique involves the application of all kinds of colour to produce special effects. The result is not always meant to be natural or suitable for normal wear. Some are excellent examples of good, wearable colour; others, however, are strong, harsh and garish effects as a fashion or styling requirement. The fantasy colourings are usually more extreme, with vivid and startling colour blends. Lighting plays an important part in the resultant colour effects and requires consideration.

Lighting has its effect on salon as well as competition colourings. Blue light produced by many types of fluorescent tube will neutralize the warm or red effects of hair colour. The yellow light of bare electric bulbs adds warmth to hair colour, and neutralizes blue or ash colour effects. 'Whiter' lights show truer hair colour than that viewed in other artificial light. Sodium street lighting will show red colours as brown.

It is necessary to consider the kind of light in which the colour of the hair is to be viewed, for example, account should be taken of the typist working under a fluorescent light for most of the day.

14.10 PRECAUTIONS

Precautions to be taken when using colour or colouring products are listed below:
(1) Always examine the scalp thoroughly for spots, cuts, inflammation, or any signs of abnormality, before applying colourings, to prevent reaction or aggravation.
(2) Choose colours wisely. The application of wrong colours undermines the confidence of the client.
(3) Use colour carefully, and do not allow the materials to be spread over the client or the equipment.
(4) Clean and replace all tools and materials after use. Check colour applicators before use. Dark colour remaining in an applicator brush could discolour light or bleached hair.
(5) Do not try to make temporary colourings do the work of permanent types. Always use products in the manner for which they are intended.
(6) Remove stains from clothes immediately with clean water. If allowed to remain they may become more difficult to remove.
(7) Use reliable products and materials which should always be correctly stored and maintained. Poor quality products result in loss of time, effort, money and clients.
(8) Measure quantities accurately; do not rely on guesswork.
(9) Test for skin reactions before colour applications. Strand test for resultant colour after applications.

(10) Avoid the use of metal containers, or discoloration of the hair may result.

(11) Do not ruffle the hair when pre-shampooing or when removing colourants.

(12) Protect the hands and skin by using rubber or plastic gloves, or suitable barrier creams.

(13) Remove surplus water from the hair before colour applications to prevent dilution of the colour.

(14) Keep colourings away from the eyes. Never use scalp hair colouring on eyebrows or eyelashes. Special, non-irritating, preparations are made for eyebrows and lashes.

(15) Check and use the correct volume strengths of hydrogen peroxide.

(16) Always work methodically and efficiently to produce confidence and good results.

14.11 THE CHEMISTRY OF COLOUR

Colour chemistry involves a large number of materials used to produce a range of colouring products with a variety of effects. Earlier products were limited in colour but more complicated and extensive varieties have been discovered.

Colouring products may be divided into the following groups: vegetable; vegetable and mineral; mineral.

Vegetable dyes or colourings are made from the flowers, stems or barks of various plants. Some of the earliest known and used for colouring hair, were extracted from common plants. *Henna* was produced from the powdered leaves of the Egyptian privet. In more recent times this was commonly used for 'henna packs' to add red colour to the hair. This is a harmless colouring which penetrates the hair and is often called Lawsone.

Camomile comes from the flower of the camomile plant and produces a yellow colour pigment which is used for brightening the hair. It is still used in some hair brightening shampoos and is a surface hair colourant.

Indigo, from the leaves of the indigo plant, gives a blue-black colour and when mixed with henna produces a variety of colours.

Walnut, from the pod shells of the ripening fruit, produces a yellow-brown dye of the surface, non-penetrating type.

Quassia, from the bark of the quassia tree, was used with camomile to brighten hair.

Other substances, such as sage, sumach, oak bark, cudbear and logwood have been used to produce a variety of colour shades and effects.

Vegetable and mineral colourings are a mixture of vegetable extracts and substances of mineral origin. One of the commonest is a substance known as compound henna, i.e. the vegetable henna mixed with a metallic salt, which is a surface colourant. Compound henna is incompatible with modern colouring and perming materials and must not be confused with vegetable henna.

Mineral colourings are divided into two groups: (i) metallic dyes and (ii) aniline derivatives.

Metallic dyes are surface coating colourings. These are known by the following terms: reduction, metallic, sulphide and progressive dyes. They consist of metal salts, e.g. lead acetate, silver nitrate, copper sulphate bismuth citrate, and salts of iron, nickel, cobalt, cadmium and manganese, which are acted on by various other chemicals to produce metallic hair colourings. The colours range from red to black, usually dark, with a dull lustre. They are not now commonly used but occasionally found in 'hair colour restorers'.

Incompatibility means the inability to mix without reaction. Hair coloured with metallic dye is incompatible with hydrogen peroxide, which is an ingredient of modern colouring and perming materials. If metallic-dyed hair is treated with one of these, discoloration, intense heat and complete disintegration of the hair could result.

Tests for metallic salts and incompatibles: hair coated with copper salts, when placed in a mixture of hydrogen peroxide and ammonium hydroxide will boil and almost completely disintegrate; compound henna on hair will react similarly, and lead deposits will lighten quickly. Silver deposits will not allow perming materials to penetrate and the result of perming hair so treated will be failure.

To test for metallic dyes on hair, place a small piece in a 'peroxide and ammonia' mixture, before attempting to apply colourings. If incompatible salts are present, discoloration, heat and breakage of the hair will result.

Aniline derivatives are substances used in many modern hair colourings. The distillation of coal and coal products produces many chemicals of medical and cosmetic use. Among these are the aniline derivative dyes. These produce the penetrating oxidation dyes in many permanent colourings, e.g., paraphenylenediamine, paratoluylenediamine, etc , which are used in a variety of ways.

Temporary colourings consist of large-molecule dye pigments and are not able to penetrate the hair shaft. These are made from yellow and red colourings and are generally called '*azo dyes*' or sulphonated azo dyes.

Semi-permanent colourings may be made from nitrodiamines and other chemicals, and are collectively called '*nitro dyes*'. These have smaller pigment molecules and are able to penetrate into the hair cuticle. They are not permanent and gradually wash from the hair.

Permanent colourings are made from small-molecule 'para dyes', e.g. paraphenylenediamine, which are known as penetrating oxidation dyes. They are oxidized in the cortex by hydrogen peroxide and other oxidizing agents. Collectively, the para dyes are called *synthetic organic dyes*. It is possible with these to lighten the natural pigment, melanin, and oxidize the synthetic dye, to produce a simultaneous lightening and tinting action. Although these dyes penetrate the hair as small molecules, on oxidation they combine to form larger molecules which enable the hair to retain the colour throughout subsequent washing. The synthetic organic dyes are likely to cause skin reaction, so skin tests are necessary to assess the possibility of allergy to these substances.

The earlier metallic dyes, e.g. sulphide and reduction dyes, were known as *double application dyes*. The modern permanent oxidation tints, usually mixed with an oxidant, e.g. hydrogen peroxide, are known as *single application dyes* (Figure 14.8).

14.12 HYDROGEN PEROXIDE

This chemical is one of the commonest oxidants used in modern colouring. It is mixed with the cream or liquid containing the synthetic colour pigment, which at first appears colourless, but darkens on exposure to air.

Lightening or darkening with modern permanent colourings and the use of hydrogen peroxide enables the colouring to penetrate the cuticle, the natural colour pigment to become bleached, and the synthetic colouring to be activated and deposited in the hair shaft.

To lighten natural hair colour 'up' two or three shades, a higher volume strength hydrogen peroxide should be used. If the natural colour is to be taken 'down' to a darker shade, then lower volume strengths are used. The volumes or percentage strength to use is determined by the manufacturer's instruction, the colour of the hair to be lightened or darkened, and the porosity of the hair (see Figure 14.9, dilutions of hydrogen peroxide).

Pre-lightening the hair is necessary when the natural colour is to be changed to a very light shade. A liquid mixture of hydrogen peroxide and ammonium hydroxide, or other bleaching agents, may be used. The modern colourings can lighten by several shades but cannot alone lighten to the very light tones.

Pre-softening is a technique used on resistant hair which involves the application of dilute hydrogen peroxide and ammonium hydroxide not to lighten, but to soften the hair cuticle and allow penetration of the colour pigment.

Activation of the colouring processes is aided with steamers and accelerators which have similar actions. The heat from them causes the hair to swell and the cuticle cells to lift. This allows quicker penetration of the colouring into the cortex, and a reduction of the processing time by half.

By using these steamers and accelerators, tint applications on shorter hair can be made to the whole length of hair irrespective of varying porosities of the roots, mid-lengths and points, as the distribution of heat allows even processing throughout the hair length. Applications must not be delayed or unevenness of colour could result.

14.13 ART AND COLOURING

There are similarities between colourings used in the art room and in the salon. These are based on the use of colour in its primary, secondary, complementary and contrasting forms, and the line and design in which it is used.

Colour is recognised by its hue, e.g. blue, green, red. The brightness of a colour is its intensity, e.g. bright glowing red or dull brown red, and its lightness or darkness, e.g. light warm red or dark rich red. A colour is seen as a colour by the eye which registers the reflection of light from a coloured surface and stimulates the nerves leading to the brain. A black surface absorbs most of the colour and no hue is registered. A white surface reflects a mixture of colours and is seen as white. A red surface will absorb all colours other than red.

By mixing paints of primary colours, i.e. blue, yellow and red, secondary colours, i.e. violet, green and orange, may be attained. From a mixture of the primary and secondary most other colours may be achieved. When white and black are added a variety of shade and tone is produced.

Light illustrates a range of colours when the rays of the sun are bent or refracted as they enter raindrops, are reflected from the far surface of the drop and refracted again as they pass out. The result is that the light rays are broken up into a spectrum of colours which are visible in the form of a rainbow. The colours as they pass through are bent at different angles: violet has the greatest deviation and red the least.

The colours of the spectrum are: violet, indigo blue, green, yellow, orange and red. Outside the visible spectrum other rays at the violet end are ultra-violet rays which cause skin tanning, and at the red end are infra-red and radiant rays with marked heating effects.

The spectrum may be demonstrated by passing white light through a prism so that it is refracted to form the colours of the rainbow. The different colours may be recombined to produce white light; if a disc on which the spectral colours are painted is rotated they appear to blend and are seen as white.

14.14 COLOURING HAIR

The colours used are divided into the different base shades, e.g. black, brown, red and yellow. These are toned with mixtures of other colours to produce a large variety. Most colour shade charts are arranged with a column of base shades on one side and in line with each a column of colour variations, e.g. the same depth of colour but with different tone. If ash, gold, purple or blue is added to light blonde a different colour shade is produced. The addition of warm colour (e.g. red, gold or yellow), or cold colour (e.g. green and blue), to base shades produces an almost endless variety. Ash shades may be produced with the addition of blue and matt shades with the addition of green. Gold shades are produced with added yellow, warm shades with red, and purple or violet tones are produced with a mixture of red and blue. The shades produced by the different colour mixtures are invaluable to the hair colourist.

14.15 TINTING FAULTS AND CORRECTIONS

Patchy and uneven colour after tint application
(a) insufficient coverage or application of tint
(b) sections too large
(c) overlapping, causing colour build-up in parts
(d) underprocessing; not allowing full colour to develop
(e) use of spirit setting lotions which may remove colour.
Correct by spot tint applied to light areas, and balance.

Resultant colour too light
(a) too light or insufficient colour in chosen shade
(b) peroxide strength too low to allow full development
(c) underprocessed, or hair too porous to hold colour.
Correct by choosing darker shade; check 'peroxide'; prepigment.

Colour fade after two or three shampoos
(a) bleaching effects of the sun
(b) underprocessed
(c) harsh physical treatment, e.g. brushing, sand and sun
(d) poor condition, too porous.
Correct by reconditioning before next tint application; process correctly; do not continually comb through.

Colour too dark after application
(a) colour choice too dark.
(b) overprocessing
(c) poor condition, porous hair
(d) possible incompatibles present, make tests.
Correct by using colour reducer as recommended.

Scalp stain
(a) very dry skin before tint application
Correct by removing with spirit, or special stain remover, or tint; cream or oil skin before subsequent tinting.

Hair too red
(a) 'peroxide' strength too high
(b) if pre-bleached, wrong choice of neutralising colour
(c) not bleached light enough.
Correct by applying matt or green colour to neutralise red effects.

Scalp irritation or skin reaction
(a) not cleanly shampooed, tint still present
(b) result of too high volume 'peroxide' being used
(c) bad combing and tint application, too harshly done
(d) possible reaction to tint chemicals.
Give no treatment. Send to doctor and notify insurance company.

Discoloration of hair
(a) poor condition, too porous, not holding colour
(b) repeated combing of undiluted tint through the hair
(c) possible reaction to incompatibles; test
(d) green colour – possibly the effect of blue ash shades on yellow base; possible reaction to metallic salt.
Correct with the use of warm or red colour but beware of producing dark brown.
(e) Mauve colour – possible incompatible reaction.
Correct with contrasting colour or remove with colour reducers.

Good colour coverage except for grey or white hair
(a) Hair resistant.
Correct by pre-softening or using lighter shade with higher volume peroxide.

Hair resistant to tint
Correct by pre-softening; using higher volume peroxide, increase processing and development time.

14.16 BLEACHING

Bleaching is the process of lightening the natural colour pigment of the hair. The effect of the chemical action is to alter the melanin from a coloured to a colourless pigment. The process is one of oxidation, e.g. the addition of oxygen from an oxidant to the chemicals in the hair.

Bleaches are made in various forms: liquid, cream or powder.

Oil bleach contains ammonium hydroxide and a sulphonated oil, e.g. Turkey red oil, as its main ingredient. This is mixed with hydrogen peroxide to form a viscous liquid. Several types are made, some intended to lighten only, others to lighten and add colour tone to the hair, e.g. warmth, gold, silver or blue.

Figure 14.8 a summary of hair colourings

Product	Uses	Duration	Development time	Other factors
Temporary rinses	Tones grey and bleached hair	One shampoo	Immediate	Colour introducer
Setting lotion	Colour tones	One shampoo	Immediate	Colouring and setting aid
Sprays and lacquers	Colour dressing aid	One shampoo	None	Dressing aid and colour introducer
Crayons	Theatrical effects	One shampoo	None	Special effects
Glitterdust	Dressing highlights	One shampoo	None	Colour, dressing aid, ornamental
Semi-permanent: rinses and shampoos	Colours and cleans	6–8 washes	5–15 mins	Longer lasting full colour
Permanent: cream, liquid, oil-based oxidation	Adds colour and lightens, tones bleached hair	Grows out	30 mins approx.	Permanent, fashion, special and a variety of effects.

Liquid bleach may be a simple mixture of 1ml of ammonium hydroxide to 20-50ml of hydrogen peroxide. Too much 'ammonia' will redden the hair. The quantities needed depend on the shade required.

Powder bleaches are made from magnesium and sodium carbonate powders which are mixed with oxidizers, e.g hydrogen peroxide, sodium bromate or perborate, and stabilisers such as sulphuric and phosphoric acids, glycerine and ethyl alcohol, together with alkaline ammonium hydroxide and sodium acetate.

The formulations vary but usually white or blue powder forms a creamy paste when mixed with oxidants. This was commonly called 'white henna' but has no relationship or comparison with vegetable henna. The paste or cream bleaches have the advantage of staying where placed on the hair. The material does not run and so cause overbleaching. Results are speedily achieved and with the many additives do not produce too warm or red a colour, or irritate the skin.

Hydrogen peroxide (H_2O_2) is one of the most commonly used chemicals for hair lightening. It has many of the properties of an acid, and is often listed as such, but it is not an acid. It is capable of releasing a large quantity of oxygen which is vital to the oxidation process of lightening. Its effectiveness is increased by the addition of an alkali, e.g. ammonium hydroxide.

Apart from bleaching, hydrogen peroxide is used in hair colourings, pre-lightening and pre-softening treatments, the removal of some colourings, permanent waving normalisers, and in lightening shampoos and rinses.

It may be purchased in different volume strengths, e.g. 10, 20, 30 and higher volumes. The higher the volume strength the larger the amount of oxygen available. From 1 litre of hydrogen peroxide of 20 volume strength, 20 litres of free oxygen may be liberated. It is dangerous to use too high volume strengths on the hair or the head, severe burns and hair breakage could result. The volume strengths given in Figure 14.9 may be obtained from 100, 60, 40, 30 and 20 volumes by diluting with distilled water.

A peroxometer, a type of hydrometer, may be conveniently used to test the volume strength of hydrogen peroxide Unstabilised hydrogen peroxide may lose its strength or efficiency if unstoppered and exposed to air and dust, which could slow its lightening action.

It is now becoming common for hydrogen peroxide to be expressed in percentage rather than volume strengths. Percentage strength refers to the number of grammes of hydrogen peroxide in 100 grammes of solution. A 6 per cent solution contains 6g of hydrogen peroxide and 94g of water.

Hydrogen peroxide may be purchased in different percentage strengths, e.g. 3 per cent to 30 per cent, 3 per cent H_2O_2 being equal to 10 volume strength and 30 per cent is equal to 100 volume strength. From 1 litre of 3 per cent hydrogen peroxide 10 litres of free oxygen may be liberated, which is the same as 10 volume strength hydrogen peroxide.

Figure 14.9 **dilutions of hydrogen peroxide**

Volume (H₂O₂)	Parts (H₂O₂)		Parts water	Volume produced
100	3	+	2	60
100	2	+	3	40
100	3	+	7	30
100	1	+	4	20
100	1	+	9	10
60	2	+	1	40
60	1	+	1	30
60	1	+	2	20
60	1	+	5	10
60	1	+	11	5
40	3	+	1	30
40	1	+	1	20
40	1	+	3	10
40	1	+	7	5
30	2	+	1	20
30	1	+	2	10
30	1	+	5	5
20	1	+	1	10
20	1	+	3	5
20	1	+	7	2.5

Various percentage strengths may be obtained by the dilutions as listed in Figures 14.10 and 14.11.

Ammonium hydroxide is produced when ammonia gas is dissolved in water. It is a valuable alkali. It is used with hydrogen peroxide to assist in lifting the hair cuticle, and in the penetration of the bleaching agent.

Ammonium hydroxide may be purchased in various strengths, the strongest being 0.880, i.e. the specific gravity of the solution. This must be diluted before applying to hair or lightening mixtures, e.g. 1ml to 20-50ml of hydrogen peroxide. Always store this chemical in a cool, dark place to prevent decomposition. Make sure it is well stoppered to contain the dangerous gas or fumes.

Figure 14.10 **dilution of 30% (100 vol) hydrogen peroxide**

30% H_2O_2 ml		H_2O ml		percentage dilution		
10	+	90	=	3%	or	10 vol
20	+	80	=	6%	or	20 vol
30	+	70	=	9%	or	30 vol
40	+	60	=	12%	or	40 vol
50	+	50	=	15%	or	50 vol
60	+	40	=	18%	or	60 vol
70	+	30	=	21%	or	70 vol
80	+	20	=	24%	or	80 vol
90	+	10	=	27%	or	90 vol
100	+	0	=	30%	or	100 vol

14.17 PREPARATION FOR BLEACHING

Place the following tools and materials in readiness for use: rubber gloves and other protective coverings, bleaching agents, glass containers, applicators and perhaps a timer. Metallic tools or containers should not be used with oxidising agents or the metal will become corroded and the hair discoloured.

Sectioning is similar to that required for tinting. Generally the thicker the bleaching agent, the smaller the sections should be. Liquid bleach penetrates a larger hair section more easily than does paste bleach. Smaller sections are required for oil bleach, and the smallest sections for cream and paste bleaches.

Application of the bleach will vary. Generally, the less porous parts are treated first. It is important not to overlap previously bleached and more porous parts of the hair. To prevent this, olive oil, cold cream, or Vaseline may be applied to the demarcation line, i.e. the line between regrowth and previously bleached hair. Uneven applications result in patchy colour. All applications should be evenly, thoroughly and correctly carried out for the best results. On completion of application, check the hairline particularly about the ears, to ensure full coverage.

Overbleaching is caused by using too high a strength of 'peroxide', processing too long, overlapping applications, combing bleach through lightened hair and lightening too-porous hair. This results in hair becoming brittle, broken, spongy, very porous and unevenly coloured and makes further colouring, toning, perming and management difficult (Figure 14.12).

Figure 14.11 **hydrogen peroxide dilution table**

% Strength (H_2O_2)	Parts H_2O_2	+	Parts H_2O	% Strengths produced
30	3	+	2	18
30	2	+	3	12
30	3	+	7	9
30	1	+	4	6
30	1	+	9	3
18	2	+	1	12
18	1	+	1	9
18	1	+	2	6
18	1	+	5	3
12	3	+	1	9
12	1	+	1	6
12	1	+	3	3
9	2	+	1	6
9	1	+	2	3
6	1	+	1	3
3	1	+	2	1

Examples

30 ml of 12% (40 vol) H_2O_2 + 10 ml H_2O = 40 ml 9% (30 vol) H_2O_2

20 ml of 9% (30 vol) H_2O_2 + 10 ml H_2O = 30 ml 6% (20 vol) H_2O_2

20 ml of 12% (40 vol) H_2O_2 + 20 ml H_2O = 40 ml 6% (20 vol) H_2O_2

Overbleached hair when wet resembles chewing gum, and the resultant shape of setting or blow styling is soon lost. The keratin structure is so weakened that a little tension causes the hair to break. Bleached or lightened hair should be treated with conditioners before further chemical processing takes place.

Removal of lighteners after bleaching should be carefully and gently carried out. The hair cuticle, particularly if overbleached, may be raised, roughened and easily tangled. The hair should be moved gently and rinsed carefully with cool, never hot, water to prevent further softening and tangling.

Special conditioners and anti-oxidants, i.e. substances used to stop oxidation, should be used to neutralise the chemical action of oxidants.

Fig 14.12 *effect of overbleaching*

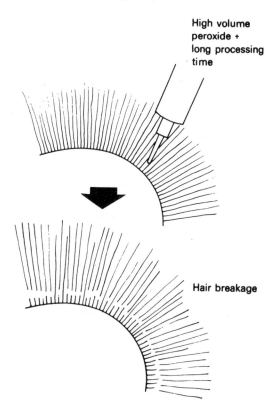

High volume
peroxide +
long processing
time

Hair breakage

These contain cuticle-smoothing properties which enable the hair to be easily combed and managed. Some of the chemicals in these products help to counteract the alkaline effects of bleaches.

14.18 THE BLEACHING ACTION

When lighteners are mixed and applied, the ammonium hydroxide or alkali content cancels out the effect of the stabilisers, sulphuric and phosphoric acids. This allows the hair cuticle to swell and the chemicals to penetrate. The released oxygen is then free to act on the natural colour pigments. The darker pigments, black and brown, are acted on first and the hair becomes lightened. Further oxidation acts on the red and yellow pigments. The degree of lightness attainable depends on how much dark and red pigments are present initially (Figure 14.13).

Fig 14.13 *bleaching action*

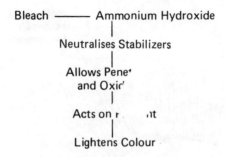

Very dark hair contains large amounts of dark pigment which may be lightened by low strengths of 'peroxide'. This leaves the warmer, red pigments unaffected, which makes the hair appear red. It may be necessary to use higher volume strength oxidants, or repeated oxidising processes, to lighten the dominant red pigments.

To reduce black hair to a very light 'white' or platinum shade, the hair should be bleached as light as possible. The remaining light yellow colour may be neutralised with a suitable toner, e.g. preferably a violet colour. Before this drastic lightening is attempted the hair should be tested, e.g. a strand of hair treated and processed to assess the degree of lightness attainable. This will prevent a long drawn out process with unsatisfactory results.

Colour lift achieved by bleaching produces a range of shades from dark brown to very pale yellow. It is rarely possible to bleach all the hair white silver or platinum, without toning. Some very light brown and blonde hair is easily reduced to a light shade without toning, but the darker the hair the more difficult it is to produce lighter shades (Figure 14.14 and 14.15).

14.19 HIGHLIGHTS AND STREAKING

These are names given to strands of lightened hair. Small pieces are usually more effective than large, chunky ones. Used in prominent parts of the head they may be used to highlight a dressing. Also called bleached streaks.

Methods of highlighting vary. Sectioned strands of hair may be pulled through holes, carefully placed, in a plastic cap and the bleach is then applied with a brush or applicator. The cap prevents the bleach from running on to other parts of the hair. The process may be speeded by steamers or accelerators, but the treated hair must not be allowed to dry or oxidation is reduced (Figure 14.16).

Alternatively, small strands may be wrapped in aluminium foil, which retains heat and quickly achieves the degree of lightness required. The root

Fig 14.14 *light and dark peroxide effects*

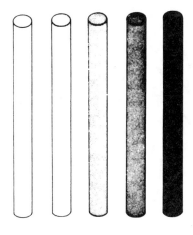

Light yellow–Gold–Darker bleached shades

Fig 14.15 *colour lift and change*

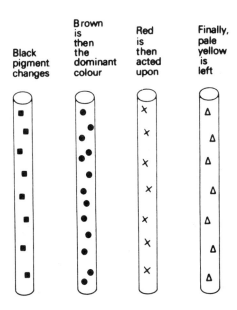

Fig 14.16 *streaking hair through a cap*

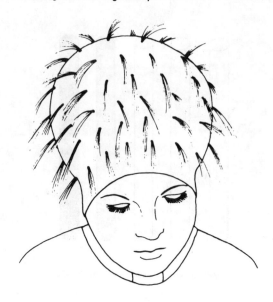

ends should be tightly enclosed to prevent bleaching of the lower part of the strand. It is not necessary to apply heat to speed the process or the bleach will 'bubble' and run to produce unwanted yellow patches on the roots (Figure 14.17).

The weave method of bleaching helps to space out the strands of hair. By taking a section of hair, the tailcomb is made to weave through, allowing alternating hair strands to be separated. This produces an effective spacing and prevents a certain amount of clumping of the strands. Better control is exercised by using this method.

Tipping, frosting, brightening, blending and lighting are terms used to describe the effects of bleaching a part, or parts, of the hair. Toners are generally used to produce a variety of colour effects, either blending or contrasting with the client's natural colour. Other effects may be produced by tinting bleached areas. There is an endless variety of effects to be produced by experimenting with a combination of bleaching, toning and tinting on different parts of hair styles.

14.20 TINTING HAIR BACK

Tinting back to a natural colour is easily achieved with modern colourings as it is easier to darken than to lighten. As a client ages, skin and hair colour are reduced. Requests for the 'natural colour' of twenty years

Fig 14.17 *streaking – foil-wrapped hair*

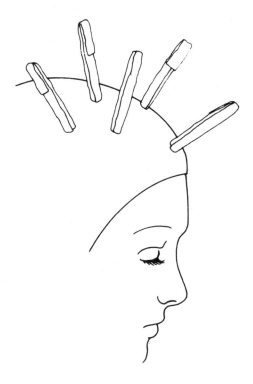

before should be met with caution: the result might well be too dark if attempted. What was the natural colour would now probably be far too dark; two or three shades lighter is more likely to be suitable. If the hair is in good condition the application may be made as for virgin hair, but if there are porous parts, colour filling or pre-pigmentation will be necessary. Putting base colour in the hair enables other colour to adhere more evenly. Red colour is commonly used, on which the final colour becomes attached.

It is usually better when tinting back to aim at a warm shade. The ashen, drab or matt shades placed on bleached hair may show a percentage of green. Pre-pigmentation colour filler should be used as recommended by the manufacturers. Any very porous ends should be cut to allow for a normal application.

14.21 BRIGHTENING SHAMPOOS AND RINSES

These are shampoos and liquids with small amounts of bleaching agent which are used to lighten hair colour slightly. A useful lightener may be made by mixing 28ml of hydrogen peroxide with 28ml of warm water, and 14ml of soapless shampoo. The quantity of 'peroxide' may be increased if a lighter shade is required.

With the ability to tint lighter with modern colourings there is often some hesitation about bleaching. Generally, if the natural colour of the hair to be lightened is dark, and very light shades are required, then it should be lightened with a bleach product first. A tint should not be made to do the work of a bleach. Although tints are able to lift one or two shades, lightening several shades is more satisfactorily done by bleaching.

The effects of sun, sand and sea, or chlorinated water, on the hair are similar to bleaching. The sun tends to dry and lift the cuticle, brushing and the abrasive action of sand roughens, and sun and salt water will slightly bleach. Hair exposed for long periods, especially if previously lightened or coloured, is particularly prone to these elements. The hair is best kept covered when exposed to strong sunlight, and sand, sea or chlorinated water should be rinsed out as soon as possible.

Testing. Where doubt exists as to the colour or porosity of the hair, always test first by applying the intended materials to a small strand of hair. Any variation of colour on the test strand may be allowed for in the final application.

Precautions to be taken with bleaches and bleaching:

(1) Apply bleaching materials evenly and use the correct volume strengths.

(2) Do not overbleach by overlapping or processing too long.

(3) Do not bleach hair previously treated with metallic or compound hair colourings.

(4) Do not allow bleach to dry out: oxidation almost ceases when the bleach is dry.

(5) Any warmth left in the hair after bleaching dark shades should be counteracted with neutralising shades.

(6) Bleach in stages, preferably with low volume strengths rather than one high one, to produce very light shades.

(7) Blue colourings or toners on yellow hair may produce green; test first.

(8) Metallic tools and containers are soon spoilt if bleaching materials are split over them; use glass or china containers.

(9) Do not bleach hair in a poor condition or in a porous state; overlapping on this type of hair results in breakage.

(10) Avoid mixing or using lighteners or colourings without first checking the manufacturer's instructions.

14.22 TONING

Toning is the process of adding colour, usually to lightened hair. A variety of pastel shades may be used on very light bleached hair, but the lightest toners can only be used on the lightest bleached base. If used on dark hair the colour will be completely absorbed, and all effects lost.

Toners may be temporary, semi-permanent or permanent colourings used in a dilute form. Specially made toners for use on lightened hair are used similarly to permanent colourings. Skin tests should be made before applications.

Mixing toners depends on the type used. Those mixed with 'peroxide' require low strengths only, the use of higher strengths may produce patchy results and porous hair.

Application of toners is similar to the application of permanent colourings. Some are used by pouring on to the hair and lightly massaging in. All need to be evenly applied and any porous areas taken into account.

Development and time of processing varies according to the type of product used. Aniline derivative types require 20–45 minutes and other toners require several applications for the colour to be built up in the hair.

The toner colour range, e.g. beige, silver, rose and other pastel shades is used for its subtle-toned effects. It is important to remember that colour added to colour produces a slightly darker shade. Differing colours can be mixed together to produce a wide range of varieties. The following list gives examples and may be used as a guide:

Red on green makes brown.

Red on yellow makes orange.

Blue on yellow produces green.

Green may be cancelled out by violet and orange.

Blue on red produces violet.

Blue may be used to neutralise orange.

Violet may be used to neutralise yellow.

The colour finally produced will depend on the depth of colour in the hair to be toned and the shade of toners used.

14.23 DECOLOURING

This means the removal of synthetic colourings from the hair by special colour reducers or strippers.

Oxidation tints may be removed by reducing agents, e.g. sulphoxylate. Most manufacturers make special sodium formaldehyde colour reducers for their products, and it is preferable to use the same make of colour and stripper. An oxidant should not be used as it will tend to help the colour to penetrate rather than to remove it.

Compound henna, vegetable and mineral dyes may be removed only by special colour reducers. Hydrogen peroxide must not be used as the chemicals are incompatible.

Temporary and semi-permanent colouring may be removed by repeated shampooing and the application of spirit.

Method of decolouring. The removal of oxidation and 'para' aniline derivative dyes from the hair may be carried out as follows:

(1) First wash and dry the hair.

(2) Mix the correct colour remover, after checking the manufacturer's instructions.

(3) Apply the decolourant to the parts of the hair where colour is to be removed. This will be where colour build-up has occurred, or if too dark, the whole of the hair.

(4) Applications may be made with a brush or special dispenser.

(5) Allow the reducer to act, preferably uncovered and without heat. Processing time is usually 10–30 minutes.

(6) Where necessary, and if in accord with the manufacturer's instructions, speed the process by covering the hair with a plastic cap and placing under a warm dryer, steamer or accelerator.

(7) Thorough shampooing is necessary when development is completed, to remove excess chemicals and to neutralise their actions. If not thoroughly done the decolouring process may need to be repeated.

The 'peroxide' test should be used when the decolouring chemicals have been removed from the hair. A weak solution of hydrogen peroxide, i.e. 1 per cent or 3 volume strength, is applied to the decoloured hair. If any synthetic pigment remains it will be oxidised by this solution and darken again.

Without this test the hair could darken over the following day or two owing to the oxidising effects of the atmosphere. The use of the 'peroxide' test indicates any ineffectiveness of the decolouring process.

If the hair darkens after testing, reapply the decolourant after removing the 'peroxide' solution. Several applications may be needed to strip the unwanted colour. Colour faults and corrections are summarised in Figure 14.18.

Recolouring after decolouring treatments will vary according to the products used. Generally no other chemical processing should follow immediately, but with some products immediate recolouring may be recommended. Perming may be carried out successfully, preferably at least a week after decolouring. Where possible, perming should be applied *before* decolouring, and the lightening action of some normalisers should be taken into account.

Figure 14.18 **colour correcting – lightening and toning**

Fault	Cause	Correction
Uneven colour	Poor application. Section too large. Mixing incorrectly.	Spot bleach or recolour.
Dark ends	Underbleached or over-bleached porous ends.	Rebleach.
	Toner too dark.	Remove, use lightener.
	Overprocessed toner.	Time accurately.
	Remains of dark tint.	Remove and tone.
Too yellow	Underbleached.	Bleach lighter.
	Base too dark.	Try stronger bleach.
	Wrong toner.	Use violet or matt.
	Wrong bleach.	Use other than oil.
Too red	Underbleached.	Bleach again.
	Too much alkali.	Use blue bleach not oil.
	Wrong toner.	Use matt, green or olive.
Dark roots or patches	Poor bleach application.	Rebleach evenly.
	Toners too dark.	Remove, use lightener.
Roots not coloured	Underbleached.	Bleach again.
	Undertimed.	Apply full timing.
	'Drippy' toner.	Apply cream not liquid.
	Temperature of toner not hot enough.	Reapply as directed.
Colour fade	Overporous.	Correct condition.
	Harsh treatment.	Advise on hair care.
	Exposure.	Keep hair covered. Comb through only dilute colour.
Hair breakage	Overprocessed.	Condition.
	Incompatibles.	Test.
	Harsh treatment.	Advise.
	Sleeping in rollers, etc.	Demonstrate effects.
Discolouration	Underprocessed.	Correct development.
	Exposure.	Condition and cover hair.
	Home treatments.	Test and advise.
Tangle	Overbleached.	Use anti-oxidants.
	Bad shampoo.	Use correct movements.
	Over rubbing.	Use gentle actions.
	Over backcombing.	Reduce and demonstrate effects.

Green tones	Incompatibles.	Test.
	Blue on yellow.	Use warm or red shades.
	Too blue ash.	Use violet.
Inflammation	Skin reaction.	Seek doctor's advice.
	Torn scalp.	
	Disease.	
Irritation	Skin reaction.	Seek doctor's advice.
	Harsh treatment.	
	Disease.	
Colour not taking	Overporous.	Recondition.
	Poor condition.	
	Lacks pigment.	Pre-pigment.
	Lacquer build-up.	Remove excess.
Colour build-up	Overporous.	Recondition.
	Poor condition.	

New products are constantly being introduced which may cause the methods, conditions and aspects of colouring, lightening, toning and decolouring to vary. What was a standing rule for many years can be repeatedly altered by new ideas and by the introduction of products containing different chemicals, as a result of the research of cosmetic chemists and scientists. Many manufacturers of these products, old and new, supply instruction, advice and courses for their use, which should not go unheeded.

EXERCISES

1 What is hair colouring?
2 Which types of colouring are used to add colour to the hair?
3 Describe the types and uses of temporary hair colouring.
4 What determines the choice of a permanent colour?
5 What is the natural colour of hair?
6 Describe a skin test, and state why it should be given.
7 How often should a skin test be given?
8 What is the difference between tinting virgin hair and tinting a regrowth?
9 What is bleaching?
10 Describe the aims and purpose of hair colour removal.

HAIR CARE

15.1 HAIR CARE

Care is essential to retain normal elasticity and shiny healthy hair. It is also fundamental to good hairdressing. The condition of hair is affected by the following: what is done to the hair; what affects the hair; hairdressing processes applied and body functions.

What is done to the hair directly affects its condition. If the hair is not correctly combed, brushed and dealt with carefully then it will become dry and limp, and tend to tear and split. Poor condition hair does not reflect good hairdressing.

What affects the hair is commonly overlooked. The hair is subjected to light, wind and air. Particularly during the summer, sunshine, salt and sand if on holiday, will cause the hair to become dry and brittle. If this is added to by poor grooming further deterioration of the hair will result.

The *hairdressing processes* applied to the hair affect its condition. If there is overprocessing of perming or colouring the hair will become dull and lifeless.

The *body functions* when in normal health will produce pliable, smooth hair. If these functions are affected by ill health, or poor diet, then the condition of the hair will become poor. It is important to be able to recognise the signs of disease which is affecting the state of the hair.

15.2 CONDITIONERS

Conditioners are made in many forms and may be incorporated in other products. The best form of conditioning, and the cheapest, is good grooming: correct combing and brushing with good quality equipment. By good quality is meant well finished, polished, pliable combs with well spaced teeth. Some cheap combs have sharp, unfinished edges which tear and break the hair. Brushes need to be firm bristle, and the coarser one's hair the firmer the bristle needs to be. Avoid hard, scratchy, rough nylon bristles for repeated use.

The effect of conditioners on the hair is to smooth the hair cuticle, to prevent the hair tangling and to resist the harsh action of other chemical treatment, such as shampoos, tints or bleaches. Some conditioners are effective on the surface of the hair; others can penetrate and be effective inside the hair. The following are some of the conditioners that are used:

(a) control dressings, creams, oils, lacquers
(b) reconditioning rinses and emulsions
(c) acid and alkaline rinses
(d) restructurants
(e) anti-oxidants
(f) pH balancers.

Each of the above is designed to correct, counter or reduce the effects of a variety of poor condition causes. Many of these conditioners rely on their physical properties, others on the chemical ingredients or their effects on other chemicals that may be used on the hair.

15.3 APPLICATION OF CONDITIONERS

When applying conditioners, the type and state of the hair should be carefully considered. Fine, dry hair needs a lot of care and too much brushing and combing should be avoided. The days of brushing the hair one hundred strokes, morning and evening, are long past. This was done to remove soap scum, dirt and dust, without washing. Using the correct shampoo now avoids the deposit of scum. There are many products designed to help fine, dry hair. Setting or blow styling the hair after beer has been applied helps, also products based on eggs, herbs, vinegar and lemon are useful. Setting the hair with beer, or rinsing with dilute vinegar or lemon juice are old-fashioned but still effective conditioners. Avoid spirit based setting lotions since these will further dry the hair.

The fine, greasy type of hair is probably one of the most difficult to deal with. The change from eating light foods in the summer to a heavier winter diet often aggravates the condition and people with this type of hair usually like to eat sweets and chocolates, which makes more grease. Drinking quantities of hot, sweet liquids makes the situation worse. Regular washing is necessary, but too much could cause more greasiness and hot water should be avoided since this will stimulate more grease. Many more shampoos are now available to deal with this type of hair. Lemon and beer shampoos are helpful and rinses of cold tea help in some cases.

Whatever product is used for whatever type of hair some will be more effective than others. Trial and error is necessary in caring for one's hair,

Trial and error

but it is important that each product is used long enough for it to be effective; using once only is rarely sufficient.

EXERCISES

1 Why is hair care important?
2 How does the functioning of the body affect hair condition?
3 What are the effects of the use of different hair conditioners?
4 What are conditioners?
5 What happens to hair when a conditioner is applied?
6 What is best used on very fine, dry hair?
7 What is best used on fine, greasy hair?
8 What effect has hair grooming on hair condition?
9 How are conditioners applied?
10 What happens when hair is in poor condition?

SUMMARY OF HAIR CARE PRODUCTS

Shampoos

There are many types available (see Chapter 5).

Setting lotions

(1) Gums

Used to hold, wet or coat hair

(2) Plastics,
PVP and
other products

Leave a pliable film on the hair; wet hair thoroughly; resist effects of moisture; reduce static electricity; hold style longer

(3) Cetrimide and other products

Keep hair pliable; repair damage; reduce static; add shine

(4) Plasticizers,
moisturizers and
emollients

Combine the features of the other setting lotions.

Conditioning rinses

(1) Lemon juice or citric acid

Removes soap scum;
eases combing;
smooths cuticle

(2) Vinegar or acetic acid

Removes soap scum;
eases combing;
smooths hair surface

(3) Beer

Adds body;
helps dressing

(4) Cream rinses

Cetrimide
and other products

Ease combing;
useful after processing;
prevent damage;
smooth cuticle;
anti-oxidant;
pH balancer

(5) Other rinses: lanolin, waxes, fats and oils

Add shine;
smooth cuticle;
ease combing;
keep hair pliable

Restructurants

Rinses and lotions.

Quaternary ammonium compounds.

Repair internal hair structure;
soften hair; add shine; smooth cuticle; make hair pliable; add proteins.

Anti-oxidants

Rinses and lotions

Stop oxidation;
neutralise alkali.

Used after bleach; used after tint

pH balancers

Rinses, creams and lotions
Counteract oxidation.

Used after chemical processing.

Dressings

Control creams, vegetable and mineral oils, gels and gloss

Smooth surface; soften cuticle; retain moisture and add shine

Lacquers

Shellac – hard coating
Plastic – pliable coating

Resist moisture;
hold style longer;
smooth cuticle.

INDEX